DFW Scavenger

I0806429

Tui Snider

REEDY PRESS

Reedy Press
PO Box 5131
St. Louis, MO 63139, USA
www.reedypress.com

Library of Congress Control Number: 2022937090

ISBN: 9781681063591

Cover and interior design by Claire Ford

Cover and interior photos by the author.
Interior clip art courtesy of Pixabay and Wikimedia Commons.

Printed in the United States of America
22 23 24 25 26 5 4 3 2 1

Dedication

To Jennifer, Byron, Arthur, Ruth, and Walter:
I look forward to exploring these places with you!

Contents

Acknowledgments

Special thanks goes to my family and friends for being so patient while I wrote this book!

I'm deeply grateful to Patty Royal for her insight and input, especially with the back cover blurb.

Super-big hugs go to Naomi for making me laugh, listening to me vent, and reminding me to avoid the Fatigue Bear.

Many thanks to newsletter readers who urged me on, especially Kristine Hall, David M. Habben, and Joanne Green.

Much gratitude goes to GhostCat, who is in a special category all his own. Thanks for all the fun stuff you share with me!

And, of course, a great big shout-out goes to my Patreon supporters for their continuing encouragement: Angel Cronk, Anne Bray, Bob McIntyre, Cheryl Farrens, Connie McIntyre,

Eva Key, Gail England, GhostCat, Hugh Cameron, Ian McAllister, Jay Wall, Jessica Wilson, Julie Reeser, Ken Reed, Margaret Cameron, Michael Samyn, Michelle Tinkham, Naomi Morlan, NV Rivera, Patty Reed, Peter Cameron, Rachel Pilcher, Sandy Lopez, Sarah Twidal, Scott Wise, Tui Wise, and Veronica Arquette.

Introduction

Different type of travel

The book you hold in your hands is not your typical travel guide. It contains no addresses, phone numbers, websites, driving instructions, or detailed descriptions. Why? Because that would spoil the fun!

Reader participation required

To use this book, readers need to participate. They need to be alert, clever, and observant, searching high and low for unusual architectural details, murals, markers, and vestiges of forgotten history they might otherwise have walked past without noticing.

How the book is set up

Dallas–Fort Worth Scavenger guides you through 27 walkable neighborhoods in 12 different cities. Each section begins with a brief overview. In some cases, cross streets or other landmarks help you narrow down the region where clues are located.

Rhyming clues and cryptic photos

For each neighborhood you will find a series of rhyming clues. Each clue is accompanied by a small photograph offering a partial glimpse of the item being described. Use the clues and photos to find the described item.

Want to win? Join in!

After you solve each clue, write it in your book. If you share photos of your trip online, remember to include the hashtags: #DFWScavenger and #TuiSnider. I monitor those hashtags on Facebook, Instagram, Twitter, and TikTok to engage with you. I also host ongoing giveaways to reward *Dallas–Fort Worth Scavenger* participants. Want to win? Join in!

To win: share photos of you and the book

What I'm looking for are photos of readers using the *Dallas–Fort Worth Scavenger* book. Be creative! For details, visit: TuiSnider.com/DFWScavenger

Now what?

Once you solve all the clues in a section, take time to enjoy the shops and restaurants in that area. With eight to 24 clues in each neighborhood, it's impossible to include every item of interest in a neighborhood or town square. You will surely discover interesting things beyond the scavenger hunt along the way. But now that you're a mindful traveler, you can share your discoveries with friends and family next time you visit.

New travel mindset

Dallas–Fort Worth Scavenger is meant to inspire a different kind of travel, travel in which readers are encouraged to slow down, take notice, and make discoveries on their own. Mindful travel is a skill that can enrich a reader's life long after they are done with this book.

Historic tidbits

I learned a lot while writing this book, and maybe you will, too! When possible, I've included historic tidbits and interesting facts in the clues. If you feel more connected to North Texas after using this book, then I've done my job.

Take me with you?

My wish is for this book to take you on fun adventures. Remember to take me with along by using the hashtags #DFWScavenger and #TuiSnider when you share your travels online.

Happy travels!
Tui Snider
TuiSnider.com

Legend

1 Bishop Arts District
2 Dallas Arts District
3 Dallas Farmers Market
4 Deep Ellum
5 Downtown: Young Street
6 Fair Park
7 Freedman's Memorial Park and Cemetery
8 Jefferson Boulevard
9 Main Street District
10 West End Historic District
11 Camp Bowie Boulevard
12 Crocket Row at West Seventh
13 Fort Worth Stockyards
14 Montgomery Street

15 Near Southside
16 Sundance Square
17 Arlington
18 Carrollton
19 Decatur
20 Denton
21 Granbury
22 Grapevine
23 McKinney
24 Rockwall
25 Waxahachie
26 Weatherford

Dallas

Bishop Arts District

The Bishop Arts District bills itself as “Dallas’s most independent neighborhood,” and rightly so. This artsy district in North Oak Cliff is home to an eclectic mix of more than 60 independently owned shops, cafes, eateries, art galleries, and bars. It’s a walkable, bike-friendly neighborhood with festivals galore, everything from Mardi Gras and Bastille Day celebrations to seasonal Wine Walks and Christmas in July.

1

When you read the plaque, it does reveal
Garcia’s creation in coated steel
Was made from streetcar tracks he found
To remind how we once got around.

2

This mural suggests that we party;
It's playful but also quite arty.
Some may find the skeletons eerie,
But they are really meant to be cheery.

3

This store is here to say:
You're never too old to play.
There's no reason for you to be "board"
With many games to add to your hoard.

4

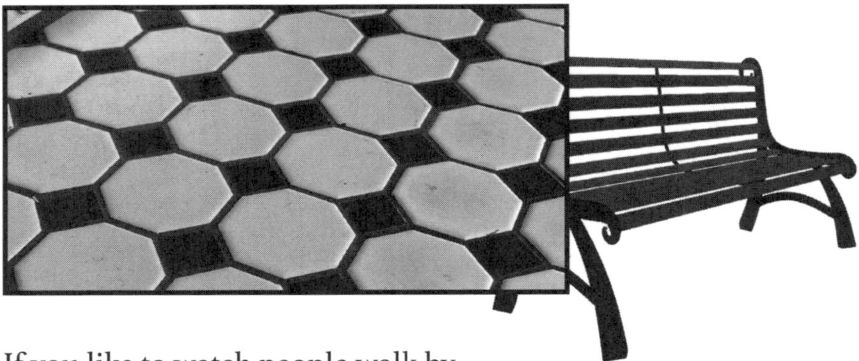

If you like to watch people walk by,
Seats are always here: give it a try.
There's a counter with black and white tile,
Set your things down and sit for a while.

____

____

5

This store is owned by a man who pens rhymes,
Selling books of essays, poetry, and crimes.
If you, too, fancy yourself a poet,
Stop by and share one: he'd love to know it.

____

____

6

This trompe l'oeil arch can really trick you:
From a distance, seems like you can step through
A historic plaque by the painted view,
Check out the marker, it's here to teach you.

7

Inside, there's so much to see,
What you buy here they'll gift-wrap for free.
Clyde Barrow hung out here, some say,
This award-winning shop's here to stay.

8

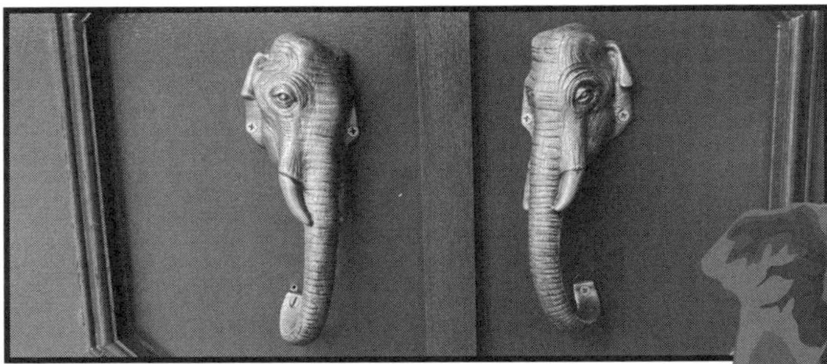

Keep an eye on doorknobs that you pass
For regal pachyderms made of brass.
The ingress itself is painted green;
The design creates a classy scene.

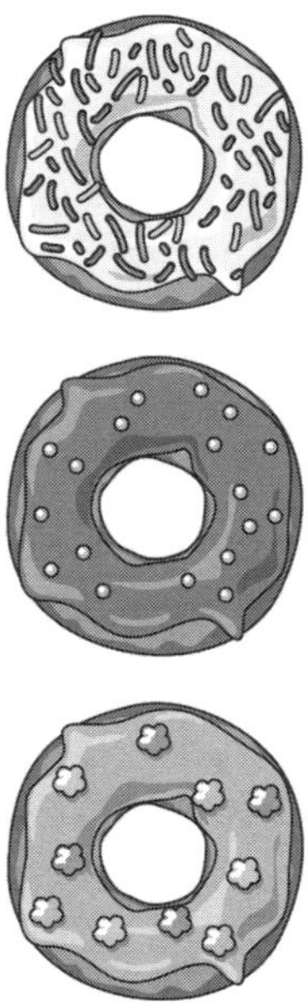

9

A festive mural in black and white,
Inside, you'll drink coffee and take a bite
Of donuts both plain and gourmet,
A gorgeous place to start your day.

10

The name makes me think of a hive,
Banding together so it can survive,
That's what creatives do in this space,
You'll enjoy browsing through this place.

11

The name's a pun for a never-married chick;
If you're an audiophile, this place does the trick.
When you crave platters for your hi-fi,
Pop into this shop and see what's to buy.

12

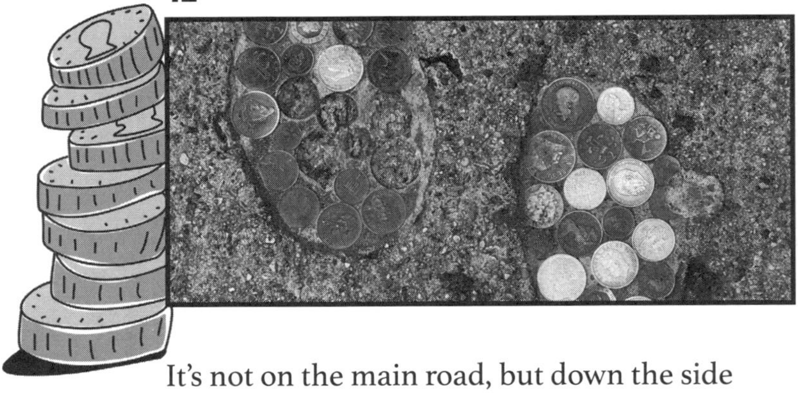

It's not on the main road, but down the side
That a strange little oddity does reside.
If you wish to see it, keep your eyes to the ground,
That's where footprints filled with coins can be found.

13

Despite what the name brings to mind,
A house of wood here you will find,
This venue's available to rent
For weddings and other events.

14

This outdoor and travel boutique
Offers items that are quite unique,
Find the big silver trailer and stop:
You'll know you've reached the right shop.

15

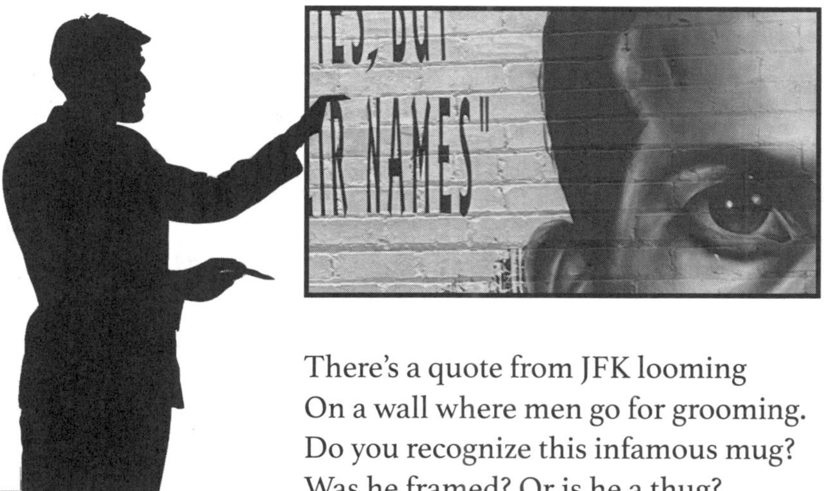

There's a quote from JFK looming
On a wall where men go for grooming.
Do you recognize this infamous mug?
Was he framed? Or is he a thug?

Dallas Arts District

In true "everything's bigger in Texas" style, the city of Dallas boasts the largest arts district in the nation. The Dallas Arts District is spread over 68 acres and is filled with venues dedicated to visual and performing arts. Throughout the year, the Dallas Arts District also hosts festivals, outdoor concerts, lectures, educational programs, and more.

1

1928 is when this building did start,
In African American history, it's played a part.
What started as a club for men and boys
Is now a dance theater for all to enjoy.

2

A Celtic cross of stone
Casts a shadow, all alone,
Guinness and whiskeys fit the style
Of this bar, themed for a famous isle.

3

Don't confuse her with a mule
As she rears up by a performing arts school.
This winged horse symbolizes the Big D,
And one of her nicknames is "Peggy."

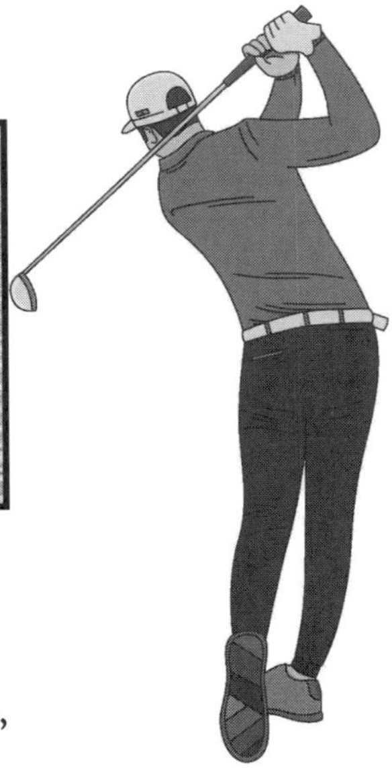

4

Live music where local artists play
Happens weekly outside the Center Cafe,
Food, music, and games create quite a scene,
There's even a mini golf putting green.

5

Silver humanoids gaze toward the sky:
Do they hope a spaceship will come by?
In any case, there's no need to be aloof,
There are cocktails and food near this roof.

6

Are these black shapes abstract guitars?
Could it symbolize music wafting to the stars?
While you stop to look along the way,
Post a selfie and see what others say.

7

This black bird is large and oh, so sleek,
Right down to its pointy beak.
"Corvus Mythicus" played during its reveal;
Wonder how that made the birdies feel?

8

Each year, new art hangs in this square,
You never know what you will see there.
Mini versions of past winners are displayed,
It is nice to see what others have made.

9

Beside this cathedral, you will find a shrine
To Mexico's patron saint, a lady divine.
The church has been here since 1902,
But the statue outside is relatively new.

10

He sits with hands around drawn-up knees,
From that high perch, what a view he sees.
If you enjoy modern sculptural art,
Visit the museum of which he is part.

11

These pooches always come as a pair,
By doors is where they sit and stare,
The female has a puppy, the male a sphere,
It's part of Asian tradition here.

Dallas Farmers Market

Since 1941, the Dallas Farmers Market has been *the* place to go for farm-fresh produce. On weekends, The Shed houses an open-air farmers market offering local produce and artisanal goods. Meanwhile, the 26,000-square-feet Market is open daily and houses a variety of restaurants and retail shops featuring Texas-made items.

1

A rooster, pig, and their friends
Greet you as you walk in.
Colorful sculptures made of steel
Give "The Shed" a cheery feel.

2

If fresh produce makes you say, "Yum,"
This is the place where you should come.
Its name makes it sound rather small,
But there's room here for hundreds of stalls.

3

With easy access to fresh food,
Living here could be quite shrewd
For those folks who love to cook:
The farmers market you'd overlook.

4

Right beside this design shop,
You will find a good place to stop.
Metal cacti look quite serene
At this playful, selfie scene.

5

This hall leads to a parking lot,
But it's quite an artsy spot.
One mural looks like a packet of seeds,
Plenty of options for your selfie needs.

6

Chat with your friends and take a brief rest,
The kids can play while you sit and digest.
Chalkboards and other playground toys
Are placed near these eateries for you to enjoy.

7

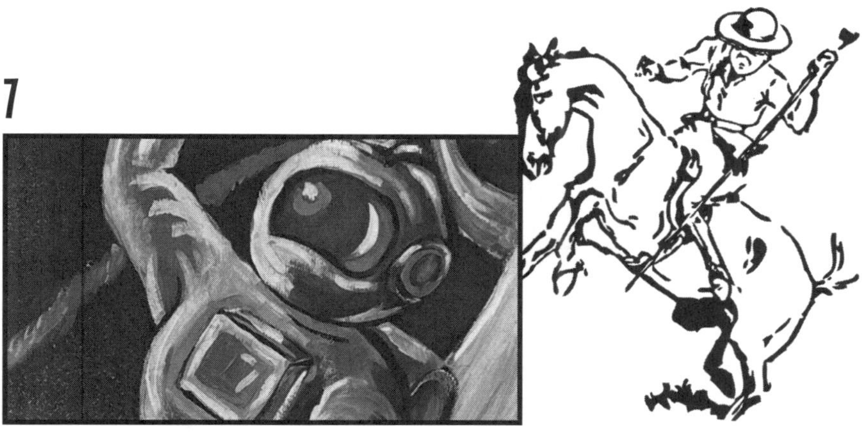

This space cowboy is getting rowdy
Riding a banana, so give him a howdy.
The artwork is rather surreal,
With a funny, but dreamlike, feel.

8

It's creative rather than exciting,
Crushed cans here are used for siding.
The design looks like the scales of a fish;
You could try this at home, if you really wish.

9

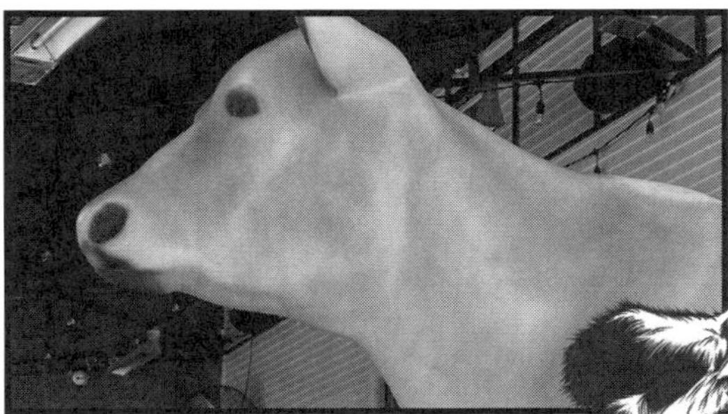

This unusual water feature
With a bovine as its creature.
No one will ever churn butter
With the liquid from these udders.

10

This tropical fruit made of brass
Adorns an entry through which to pass.
Once inside, it is time to order
Cuisine from south of the border.

11

When you see this vehicle of red,
You're at the market and not The Shed,
Common on farms, it stands out in the city,
Its only job here is to look nice and pretty.

Deep Ellum

Deep Ellum originally was a freedmen's town, founded by former slaves just a mile east of downtown Dallas. In the 1920s, it became a mecca for jazz and blues, and hosted many famous acts from that era, including Blind Lemon Jefferson and Bessie Smith. Today, Deep Ellum is still known for its arts and music scene, along with an eclectic mix of nightclubs, shops, and cafes.

1

Maneki-neko beckons to all
From a mural on an outside wall.
The food inside is decidedly Asian;
Once you taste it, you won't need persuasion.

2

If you crave nostalgia or wacky gifts,
This funky store will give you a lift,
They carry over 400 types of soda,
There's even candy that looks like Yoda.

3

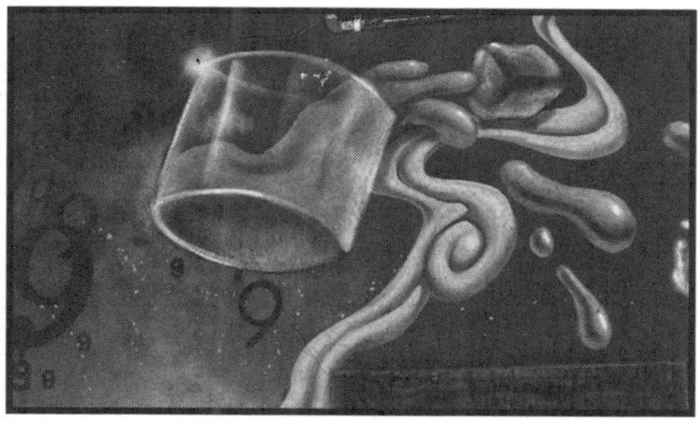

In a blue suit, a feline looks dapper,
Inside, at night, you may hear a rapper,
A patio overlooks the street;
Artists sometimes come here to meet.

4

“Big things happen here” is the rallying cry
You are meant to feel as you walk by,
If between the letters you take a stance,
You spell the word “Big:” it’s not by chance.

5

Snap your picture here, and it could
Serve to make someone else feel good
When they read the simple phrase:
Three words can brighten up their days.

6

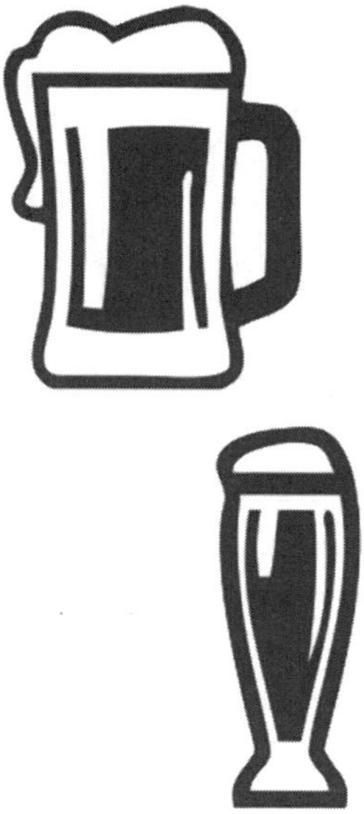

At the corner of Elm and Malcolm X
Stands a new bar, let's wish them success.
A mural here looks like the wall is peeled,
And inside, a colorful life is revealed.

7

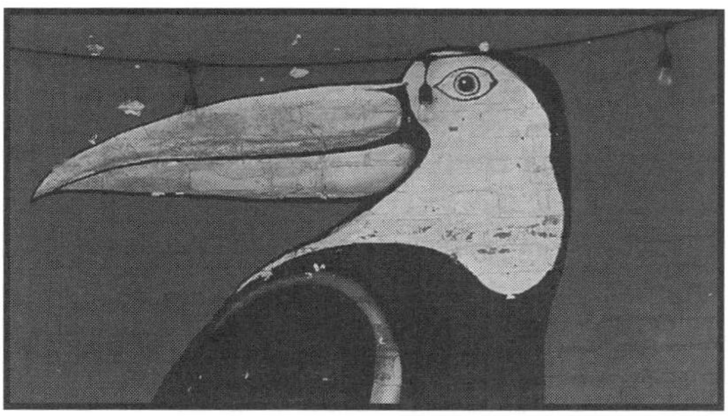

This mural's been here since '94,
With a happy toucan above the door.
Inside, there's coffee and food
That's sure to lift your mood.

8

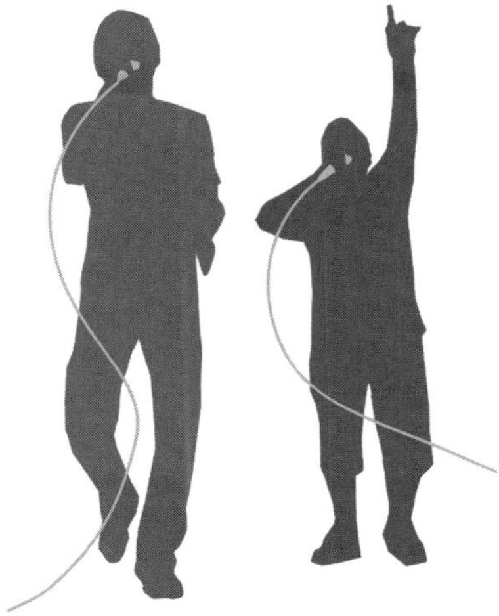

Named after a rebellious style of art,
This club in the '90s got its start,
From the doorway, colorful faces leer,
At night, they play live music here.

9

A steampunk vibe can be found here:
The front door features metal gears.
It's not a welding shop, if that's what you think,
Instead, it's a bar with food and drink.

10

Many recordings have been made
Of this blues song over the decades.
The marker gives historic narration;
Visit YouTube to hear variations.

11

If he's backlit, you may have to squint
As you search around for Clint.
This mural is near a parking lot;
Peek over a fence: that is the spot.

12

On bricks, find this pale ghost sign,
It's for a famous moving line.
If solving this clue is going slow,
Look for tacos and coffee for sale below.

13

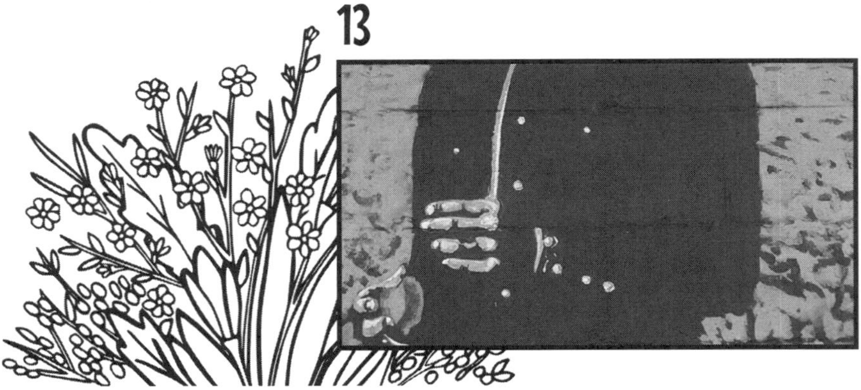

He stands in a bluebonnet field,
Music is what he does yield,
On the streets is where he started,
But now, Charley's tunes have charted.

14

Several murals are near this sushi shop,
It makes an intriguing photo op.
From a girl in stripes to a mystic kitty,
You can take a picture that is pretty.

15

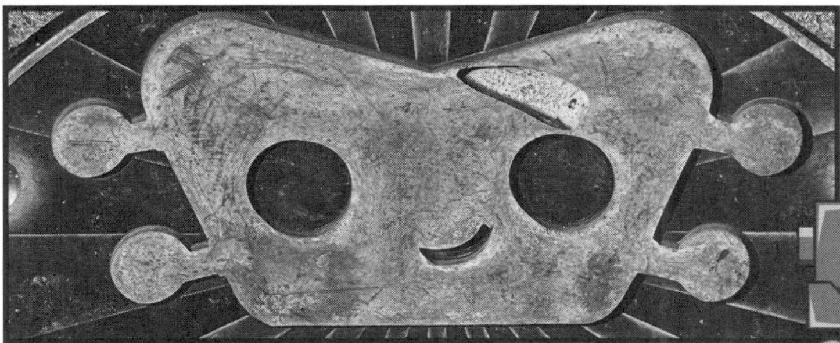

A trio of robots and birds
May sound a little absurd.
This unique, brushed steel art
Was commissioned in '07 by DART.

Downtown: Young Street

On this walkable stretch of Young Street, running from Pioneer Plaza to City Hall, you can find sculptures, water features, a memorial, and even a historic cemetery in the shadow of skyscrapers. (Free street parking is available at Pioneer Plaza.)

1

Forty-nine bovines of bronze
Endlessly race across lawns
As mallard ducks quack in the pond,
Will they ever reach the beyond?

2

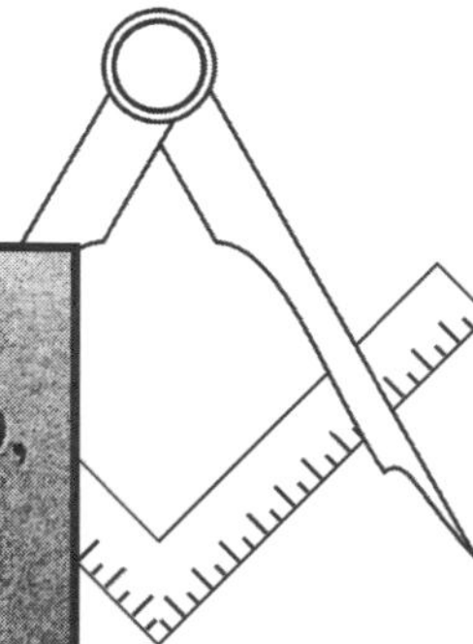

Although Darnell was born in the sticks,
He climbed military ranks and politics.
His headstone wording makes it quite plain
The grand master status he also attained.

3

After many sorrowful family losses,
She devoted herself to charitable causes.
Let us take time to remember and not forget
The kindhearted woman named Juliette.

4

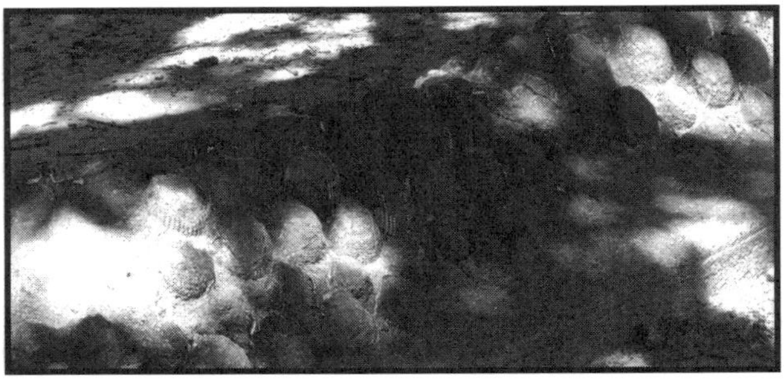

A newspaperman, soldier, and mayor
Has been laid to rest here with much care,
Not many graves here have shells atop mounds,
But it is common in historic burial grounds.

5

He joined the Odd Fellows to live up to his name:
Members strive to live good lives beyond blame.
Inside of a linked chain, three letters you'll see,
"Friendship, Love, and Truth" are what they're meant to be.

6

Look for a massive canopy of steel
With shapes cut out so it will reveal
Badge numbers, seen through shadows and light:
This unique police memorial is a moving sight.

7

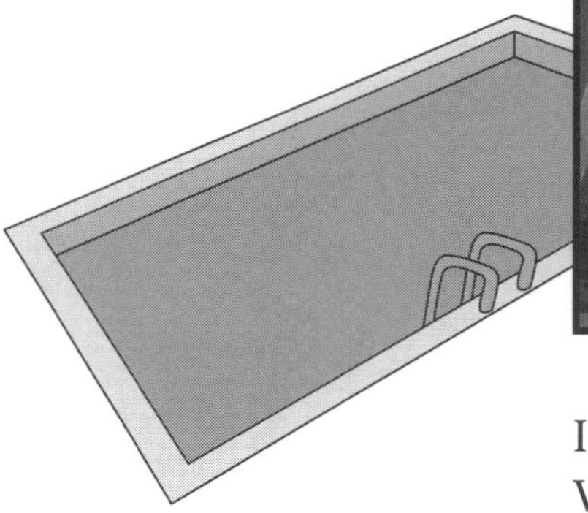

I was designed by I. M. Pei
With a reflecting pool along the way.
Recognize me from *RoboCop*?
Either way, I'm worth a stop.

Fair Park: Art Deco Buildings

Not only is Fair Park a National Historic Landmark, but every fall, it's also the site of the Texas State Fair. Fair Park features the nation's largest collection of Art Deco buildings and murals, all of which were built for the 1936 Texas Centennial Exposition. While you are welcome to explore the entire 277-acre park, the following clues focus on the Art Deco section, starting with the Hall of State and its surrounding area.

1

The original was a gift from overseas,
But this one honors the anniversary
Of Boy Scout troops across the nation;
She's a small but accurate recreation.

2

As through the Court of Honour you wander,
Words are carved in relief for all to ponder.
The very ideas of "honour" and "romance":
Finding these takes much more than a glance.

3

There is much to see at this ingress:
Texas themes are what these doors express,
Rattlers and spurs of bronze and brass,
Lone Star symbols built to last.

4

A golden warrior poses with a bow,
Look close and see there's no arrow.
Let your eyes trace a line through the sky,
He points to the Texas Seal on high.

5

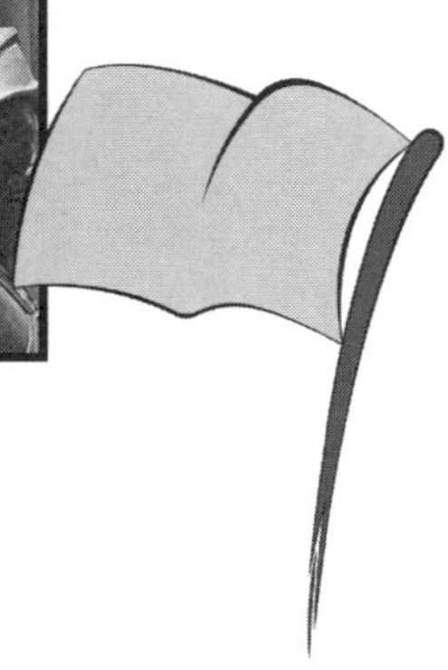

Soldiers in uniforms from around the world
Represent the six flags of Texas unfurled.
You see them if you take time to look close
At the light posts here: they are missed by most.

6

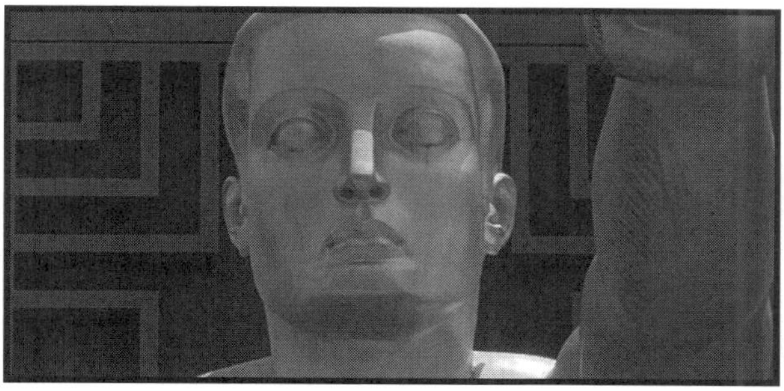

On one side a woman, the other a man,
Framing the fountain was always the plan.
When they disappeared, it ruined the design,
But they were replaced in 2009.

7

You'll see a cougar catching a bison in this scene,
Ground transportation is what this artwork means.
It was created by a French artist named Bourdelle
For the Texas State Centennial.

8

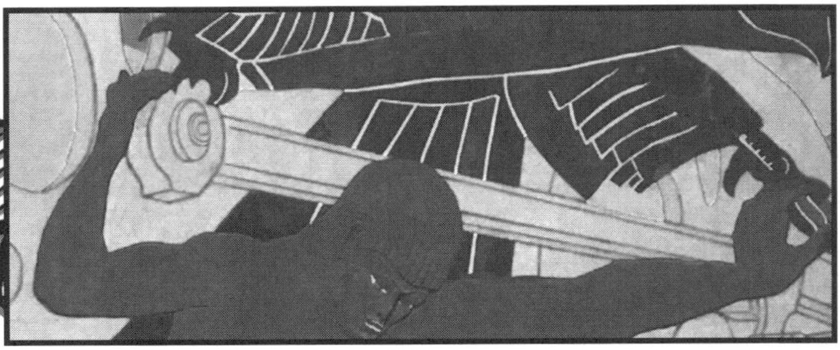

Here we see a man and eagle
In a struggle that is not regal.
It stands for humans and machines,
A conflict that must be in our genes.

9

She stands on a pedestal eleven-feet-high
The "lone star" behind her catches your eye,
A woman named Helen posed for this statuette;
She was a Texas Centennial Rangerette.

10

To the north, a statue stands for Spain,
Her scarf shows an animal known for its mane.
On her head a mantilla, and a castle in her hand
Remind us that her country once owned this land.

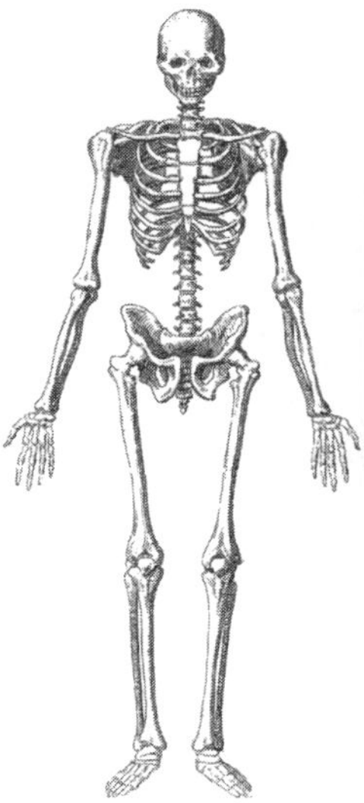

11

In 1942, these murals were damaged by fire,
They were later restored so we can still admire.
This one in the Mexico Portico does display
Images honoring the invention of the X-ray.

12

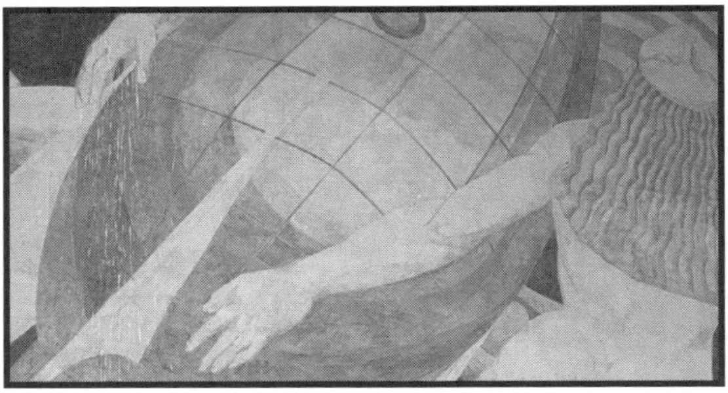

This mural with its airship streaming
Looks retro now, but its real meaning
In Deco-style oils on Portland cement:
The future of transportation to represent.

13

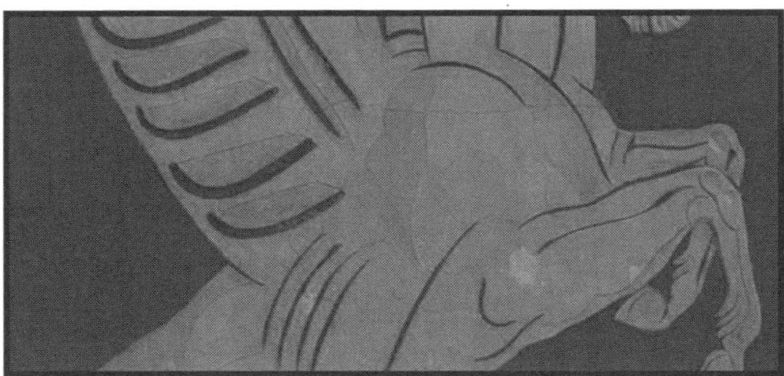

On one side Pegasus, the other side sirens,
Adorn these blue and red Art Deco pylons.
A symbol for Dallas is the winged horse,
And as you know, mermaids like water, of course.

14

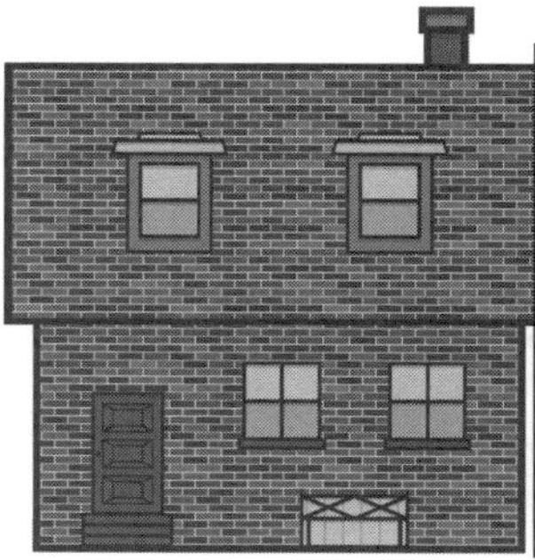

During the Texas State Fair, it's free to enter
This colonial-style house that's the DAR's center,
A club that honors America's past,
They'll share what they know if you ask.

15

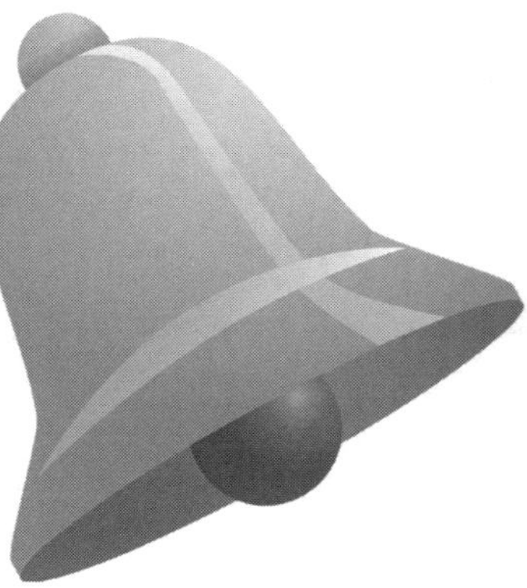

This great big bell was a gift;
It's way too heavy for one to lift.
This replica is so exact,
It even has the famous crack.

16

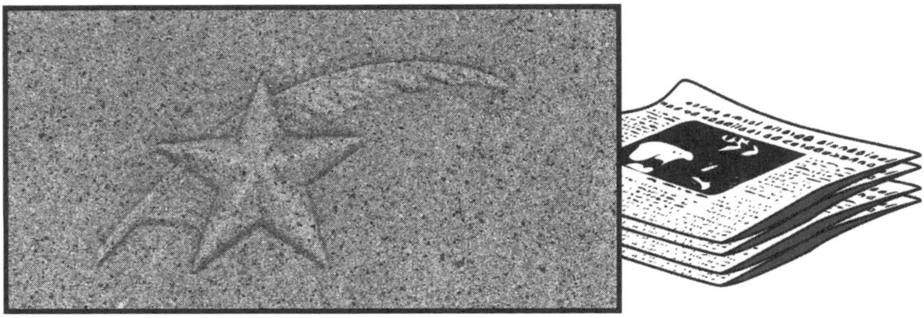

This statue thanks State Fair founders and the press,
And as a further way their gratitude to express.
Beneath lies a crypt filled with newspaper clippings
That were sadly damaged by leaky drippings.

17

This was given to the city by a club:
You can find it nestled near a shrub.
Inscribed here are the famous regulations
Taught by churches in many nations.

18

Granite tablets stand here, of which there are five,
To honor those from Texas who lost their lives
While serving in America's longest-lasting war.
They are remembered here for evermore.

____

____

19

For this, the singer "Gorgeous Georgia" did pose,
Standing on a cactus that in Texas does not grow,
The mural behind has symbols to celebrate
The centennial of the Lone Star State.

____

____

Freedman's Memorial Park and Cemetery

Freedman's Memorial Park and Cemetery was established in 1869 as a burial ground for African Americans. However, when the Central Expressway was built in the 1930s, the cemetery was all but destroyed. Descendants of those buried here have since partnered with the Texas Department of Transportation to preserve the historic Freedman's Cemetery site. The park is now a protected state archaeological landmark with a series of bronze statues, poetry plaques, and monuments throughout.

1

More than 5,000 freed slaves here once had graves
Until a major freeway over all was paved.
This plaque tells part of the story
Of how Freedman's Cemetery regained its glory.

2

The archway is framed by a woman and man;
He holds a machete, she beckons with a hand.
They both wear West African clothes
And strike a relaxed and confident pose.

3

David Newton's bas-reliefs
Express slavery's misery and tragic griefs.
A woman covering up her face
Symbolizes profound disgrace.

4

The pathway's shape, seen from above,
You'd notice easily if you were a dove,
But if you use your imagination,
You'll realize it has a cross formation.

5

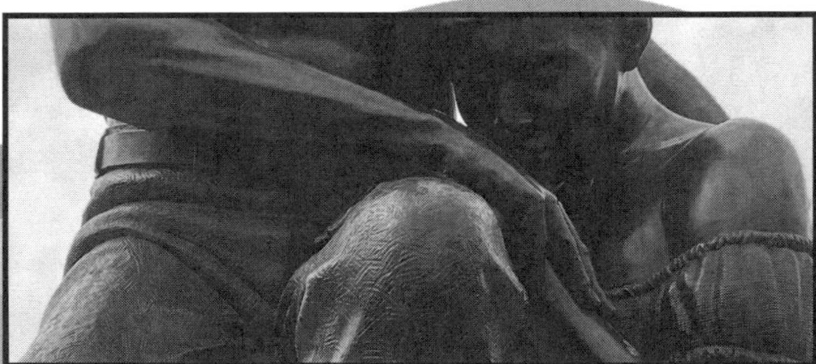

A freed couple embrace at the center
Of the path you walk after you enter.
The suffering of ancestors shapes their attitude;
They are hopeful and filled with gratitude.

6

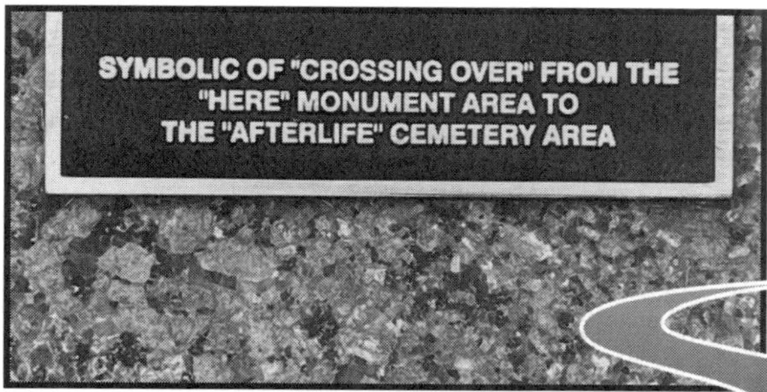

Water flows in this created riverbed,
A symbolic border between living and dead.
A granite marker sits in the grass
To explain this to all who may pass.

7

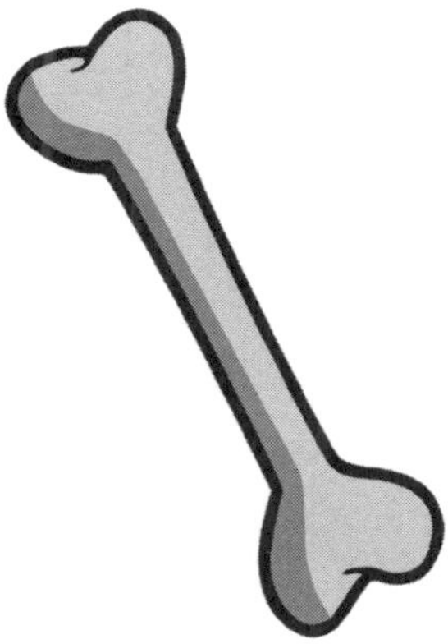

Out of thousands, only two headstones were found;
Think of all the lost stories that still must resound.
Look behind the poem "Here" to see these stones
And ponder the history of many lost bones.

Jefferson Boulevard

Home to the Oak Cliff Cultural Center and the historic Texas Theatre (where Oswald was caught JFK's assassination), Jefferson Boulevard is one of the original shopping streets in Dallas, with head-in parking, wide sidewalks, and one-story buildings. Shops here cater to the Mexican American community, so many signs are in both Spanish and English.

1

The movie playing was *War is Hell*
When Oswald snuck in for a spell.
Despite this clever hiding spot,
It wasn't long 'til he was caught.

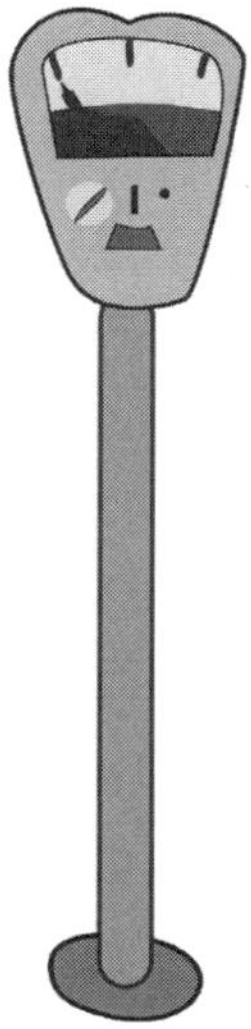

2

This artwork is brightly colored and strange;
If you park here, they may eat your change.
Standing in front of a nonprofit boutique,
Look closely, because each one is unique.

3

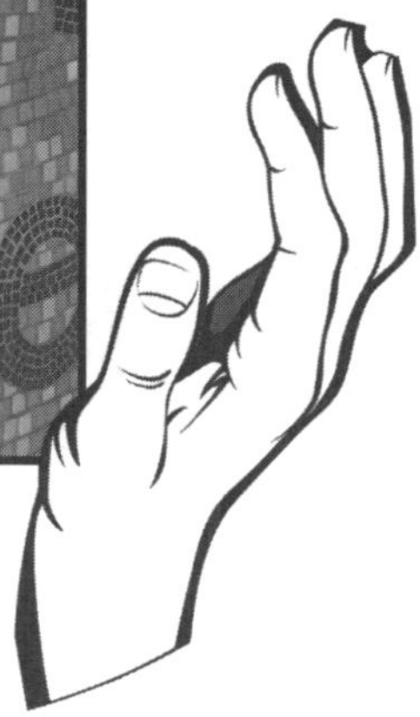

A mosaic standing nearly 18 feet tall
Features an eye in a palm that sees it all.
Students were inspired by an Indian prayer,
They even quote a line if you look carefully there.

4

You will need to glance down by your feet
To see this "ghost sign" embedded in concrete.
Jefferson Tower once housed this men's store,
They now sell cookies there, and much more.

5

When you're jonesing for food from under the sea
You can eat at this place that's run by family.
Above one door, a mermaid does beckon,
Another in the window: it's a theme, I reckon.

6

Vintage enthusiasts love this Googie-style sign,
It has a "Jetsons" feel to its design,
Above a home furnishing store erected:
Historians think it should be protected.

7

It was once a Latin music store,
The signage remains, but nothing more,
It's now a market for what's gently used,
Where discarded items can be rescued.

8

They been dishing burgers and steaks since '64,
You can smell it even before you reach the door,
From the rooftop, Sonny the steer does gaze
As if longing for a chance to come down and graze.

9

This iconic sign will remind some of Poe;
A drug store once found here is "never mo',"
Shops below may change, but it seems this raven
Has claimed this building for its permanent haven.

10

The store's font has a jaunty '60s style,
Murals on the side were made to beguile.
Together, it adds to Jefferson's flavor,
A cultural blend that visitors savor.

11

This greasy spoon is painted bright navy,
Inside, you'll find more salsa than gravy.
The name means "godfather" in Spanish lingo,
They'll feed you well, even if you're a gringo.

12

Officer Tippit came here before he was shot
By Oswald, who down the street was caught.
More than a record store, this place does its part
As a nonprofit group to promote the arts.

13

You may need to crane your neck to see
This ghost sign for a music academy.
High on a brick wall is where it sits,
Crossing the street can help you see it.

14

This mural has symbols for land, sea, and air,
A snake, fish, and eagle are painted with flair.
Its design incorporates elements of Art Deco
To honor local architecture like a visual echo.

15

Since the 1920s, this school is where
Thousands have come to learn to cut hair.
Walk-ins are welcome; that's how students learn,
The price is right, too; you won't spend all you earn.

Main Street District

Downtown Dallas is the second-largest business district in Texas, and it's got the skyscrapers to prove it. But in the midst of all the hustle and bustle, the Main Street District has plenty of historical architecture, unusual artwork, and interesting tidbits for you to discover.

1

This Main Street parking lot is now a park,
Where families play from dusk to dark.
The prairie landscape is pretty neat;
The fountain gives relief from Texas heat.

2

Since 1885, this daily news
Has done its best to share its views.
In the '20s they stood up to the KKK,
And are still in circulation today.

3

This mosaic is a sight to behold:
It features Italian glass and 22-karat gold.
Commissioned by a mayor in 1959,
Luxury apartments keep it looking fine.

4

Since 1907, they've offered luxury shopping,
And this flagship store has no plans for stopping.
Their Christmas catalogue has a wild reputation
For decadent gifts that boggle the imagination.

____

____

5

If a shortcut you'd like to attain
While walking from Commerce to Main,
Duck into this pedestrian arch.
It will save your tootsies a march.

____

____

6

This Art Deco building's an impressive sight.
Stained glass images show Thor creating light,
With busts of Edison and Steinmetz way up high;
Below, they brew beer that you can try.

7

This neo-Gothic creation
Is a five-star accommodation.
The basement bar is quite groovy,
Based on Kubrick and David Lynch movies.

8

Its namesake blossom is engraved over the door
Of this Beaux-Arts building with 29 floors.
A neon-red Pegasus flies from the roof,
A famous symbol of Dallas on the hoof.

9

This high-tech park is used night and day,
Interactive art, games, and music do play,
A public plaza to come and explore,
Check out their calendar to find out more.

10

He made a name for himself selling beer
Long before he ever came here,
For him, the city hall building was razed,
And this hotel built that continues to amaze.

11

This statue was moved from Whitacre Tower,
It brandishes lightning bolts as a symbol of power,
Called "Spirit of Communication" or "Golden Boy,"
By either name, it's here to enjoy.

12

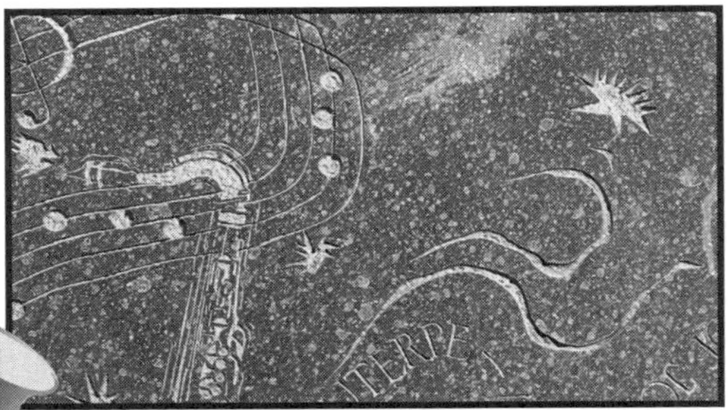

This park is named for a flying horse.
It's near the Magnolia Hotel, of course,
With a marker for Euterpe, who is music's muse,
Sometimes, for live bands, this plaza is used.

13

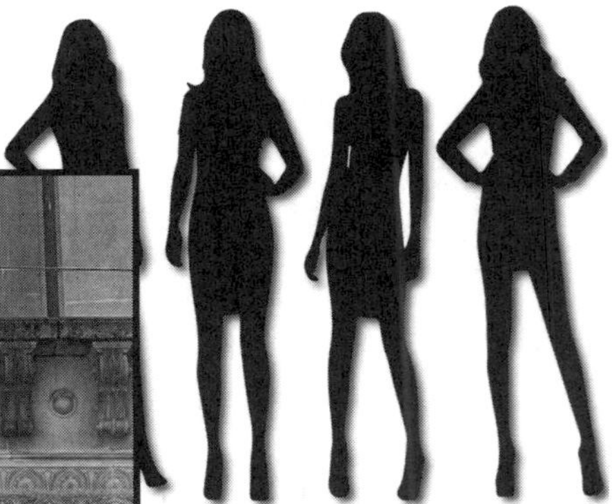

This facade holds four sultry ladies
In niches that keep them cool and shady.
They used to host Jazz-era soirees;
I sure hope it reopens someday.

14

The largest banks in the Lone Star State
Loaded bags of cash while clients did wait.
I'm sure they did not dilly-dally
While doing business in Money Alley.

15

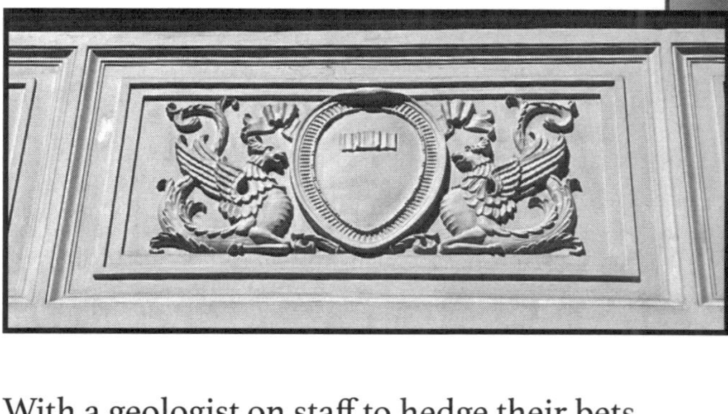

With a geologist on staff to hedge their bets,
This bank's oil boom money was as good as it gets,
Republic Bank thrived through the Depression,
But the '80s left a different impression.

16

Below this "main place"
Lies a nearly secret space:
There's an entry on this street
To shops and cafes 'neath your feet.

17

Onlookers can easily admire
Terra-cotta details and Gothic spires;
Once an annex for the Adolphus Hotel,
It now has apartments in which you can dwell.

18

Look down to see where a knight does still pose
In this entry for a shop that sold men's clothes,
Now housing legal aid: it's no longer a store,
Yet this terrazzo design remains, evermore.

19

These tiles are flat, yet they look quite 3D,
A black and white design that's clever and pretty.
People come here so their muscles can train;
When you find these, don't let your eyes strain.

20

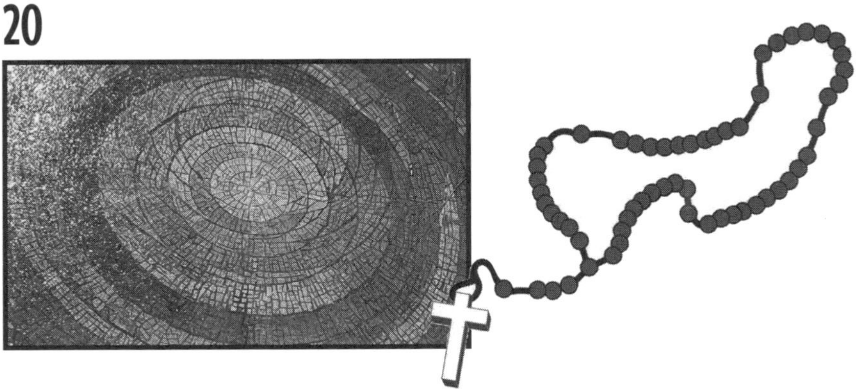

If you need a moment of peace and quiet,
It's free to stop in, there's no need to buy it,
Look for the mosaic of many colors bright
Above the doors that open to this site.

21

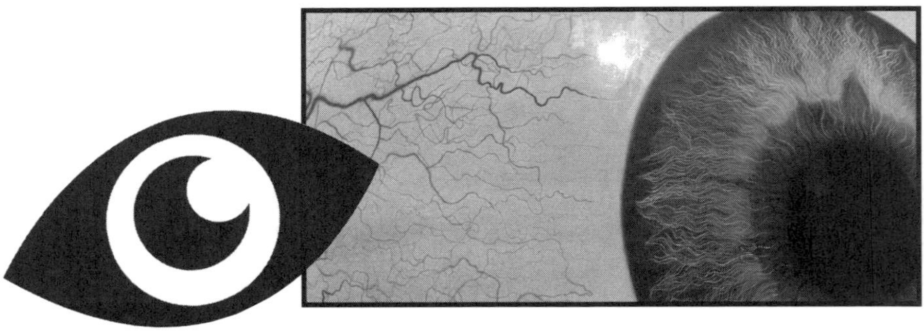

A 30-foot, fiberglass, ocular sphere
Was made in Chicago and transplanted here.
It was purchased by a billionaire:
No one quite knows why he put it there.

22

This walkway from Elm to Main streets
Is near many great places to eat,
Wander the red bricks and find some good food
Or just people-watch, if you're in the mood.

23

The tallest building in Dallas until 1909,
Inspired by an opera house is its design,
Luxurious apartments are found upstairs,
Below, Italian food is made with care.

West End Historic District

What began with a trading post in the late 1800s and later became the site of JFK's assassination is now called the West End Historic District. Several museums can be found here, including the Sixth Floor Museum and the Dallas Holocaust Museum. In addition, many historic brick buildings here have been renovated for shops, cafes, and restaurants. There's even a "smart park" where visitors can recharge their cell phones.

What was once a cement parking lot
Was transformed into a lush green spot,
Full of technical innovations,
Swings for adults and phone-charging stations.

2

From breakfast all day to dessert,
The food here is Southern comfort.
The chef named this place after his mom,
When you eat here, you'll surely say, "nom."

____

____

3

Some claim it's haunted (and it's certainly old);
The sign painted on it is decidedly bold.
What once was a giant hardware store
Now serves Tex-Mex and margaritas galore.

____

____

4

Holocaust survivors in 1984
Created a museum which, at its core,
Is intended to keep history alive,
Even painful memories need to survive.

5

Oklahomans were shocked to find it alive
After withstanding a bombing in '95.
Its branches symbolize strength and hope,
Important traits humans need to cope.

6

This is where seeing is not believing:
Exhibits here are intentionally deceiving.
Family photos can be quite confusing,
But the experience is intended to be amusing.

7

This Western retailer is not a chain store,
A longhorn skull greets you at the door.
Inside, you'll find all you could want,
If cowboy style is what you like to flaunt.

8

Their logo is literally a brand
Named for Youngs O., who was once a ranch hand.
Beef, gator, and venison are all on the menu
Of this well-established West End venue.

9

While walking brick paths by the streets,
You may smell sweet and savory treats,
You really won't have to go far,
Their name tells you right where they are.

10

The word engraved over these gates
Makes me think of palm trees and dates.
There are no camels here to be seen,
And yet this courtyard looks quite serene.

11

Many buildings here are brick,
So these two arches do the trick,
Neither Roman, nor for selling fast food,
Their style fits this neighborhood's mood.

12

This old courthouse was once a museum,
Its cornerstone filled with items (you can't see 'em)
Red sandstone bricks, pointy spires, and modest height,
Make this Romanesque building an eye-catching sight.

13

Five solemn slabs of black granite
Remind us of what we take for granted,
So take time to stop as you wander,
Read the names engraved here and ponder.

14

A man came from Tennessee
And founded what we call the Big D.
This cabin is similar to the house
He shared with five kids and a spouse.

15

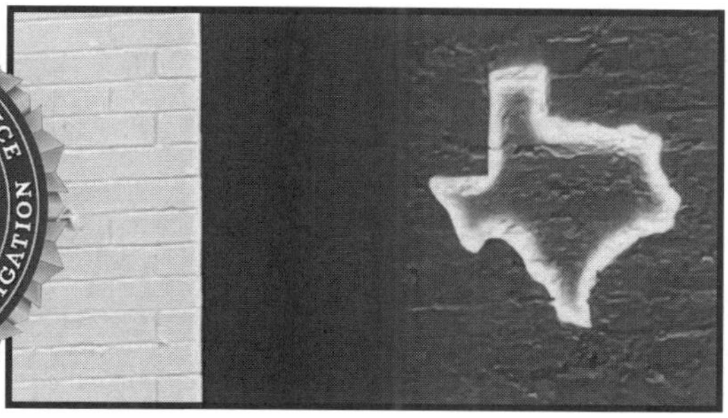

Some claim this is where Bonnie met Clyde;
She waitressed, while he dined inside.
Modern regulars include the FBI,
Who come to munch on burgers and fries.

16

After America's president was shot,
The FBI set up shop in this spot
Named for a family, not a gal's bag,
That's a nickname this building still has.

17

This museum is the scene of a crime
That changed the USA for all time.
It's from here that Oswald took aim;
The president's life he did claim.

18

Built in the 1930s with Art Deco style,
This park in Dallas was meant to beguile,
But its reputation is permanently scarred
By events in '63 that in this area they marred.

19

This cenotaph stands 30 feet high,
A meditative place 'twixt earth and sky,
A space to release tragedy and strife
And remember this president's too-short life.

Fort Worth

Camp Bowie Boulevard: Penticost to Hulen

While it's worth driving the entire length of Camp Bowie Boulevard, the stretch from Hulen to Penticost streets is a walkable place to start. This section still boasts distinctive red bricks from the ghost town of Thurber, Texas. There's plenty of Fort Worth history to find here, from the oldest restaurant in town to overlooked architectural details with ties to the past.

1

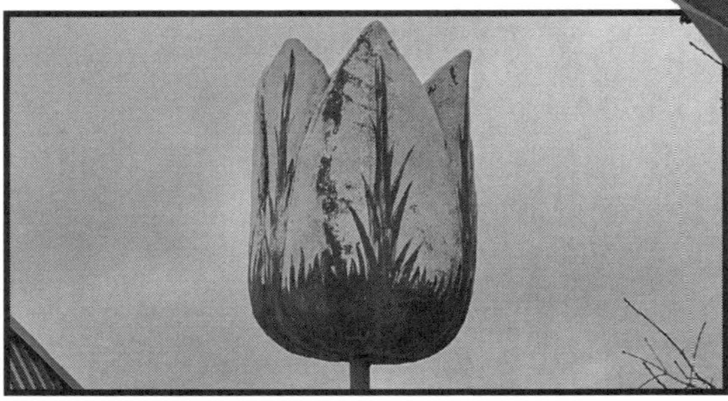

It's so tall that it catches your eye
Every time you pass it by.
Who planted this gigantic flower?
Its conspicuous look gives it some power.

2

Their name recalls a Greek myth,
But it's only stains that they lift,
Their handmade goods will enhance your decor,
If you buy one, you will surely want more.

3

This dive bar is haunted by locals,
If you're new here, you'll be noticed by yokels.
The signage looks like it's from the Old West,
Only 21-and-overs can be their guests.

4

This burger joint keeps it old-school,
They grind their own meat daily, as a rule;
As you enter, retro vibes and bench seating
Add to the fun of all that you're eating.

5

From cowboy styles to haute couture,
This store's offerings are a fashionista lure,
Each item is so thoughtfully chosen,
You'll look glam in whatever you pose in.

6

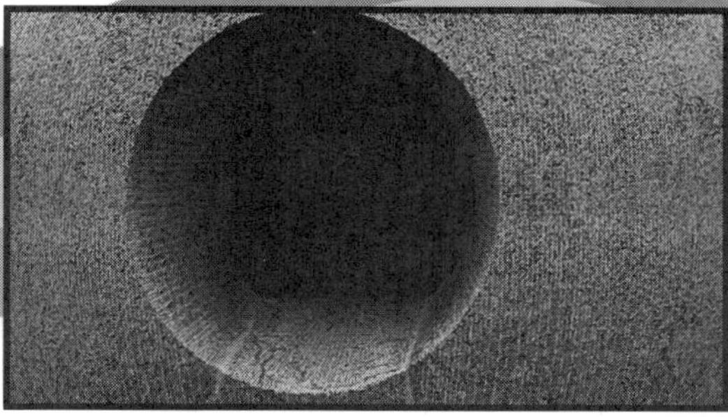

Klinefelter's granite sculpture can be seen
In a pocket park called Byers Green.
It looks best when its water is flowing
And the zigzag path has grass nearby growing.

7

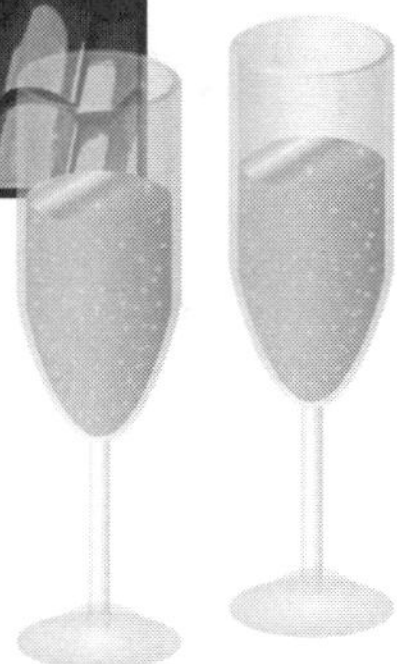

The menu will satisfy your mood
For classically-tasty American food,
From date night to Sunday brunch:
It's a mainstay for dinner or lunch.

8

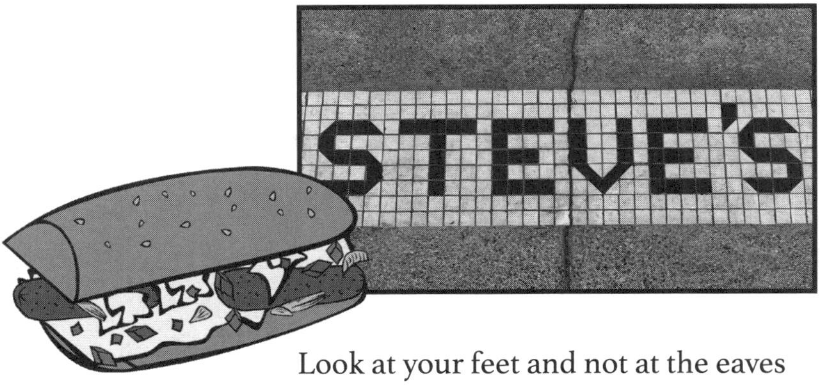

Look at your feet and not at the eaves
To find this overlooked reference to Steve's,
A popular cafe from many years before;
His ham sandwiches are culinary lore.

9

It's the oldest restaurant in town
Serving Tex-Mex of high renown.
It was once FDR's favorite venue:
His special meal is still on their menu.

10

Those of us who work from home
Know at times you can feel alone,
This cafe has office space to rent:
Even for a break, it could be heaven-sent.

11

Named for our state flower, it's not a hat,
In a brick building is where it's at,
Fresh-baked goods since 1934,
Pastries, cakes, and petit fours.

Camp Bowie Boulevard: Ridglea Village

This section of Camp Bowie Boulevard is no longer paved in brick, but it's still full of interesting sights. The Ridglea Village shopping center is a good place to explore. From the historic Ridglea Theater and its stone tower to unusual landmarks and independent shops, you can easily while away an afternoon with friends and family.

1

Perched on a rooftop for 25 years,
Is it a rabbit or is it a deer?
Each time the business below changes hands,
The creature above it remains where it stands.

2

Saved from demolition and locally adored,
With a 70-foot tower, this landmark restored
Continues to stand tall along west Camp Bowie
With the same look and feel as the 1940s.

3

You won't get tetanus here, despite the name,
Street tacos and margaritas are their game,
There's TV inside, but there's outdoor seats, too,
Dine al fresco, and you can bring Fido with you.

4

This Rolex won't fit on your arm,
But it still has plenty of charm.
As you pass by on the busy sidewalk,
You can tell time from this very large clock.

____

____

5

Named for the pastry that inspired Proust to write,
This venue is guaranteed to delight.
You may learn French while washing your hands,
But here in Texas, not all understand.

____

____

6

Folks come here to look and feel better
With infrared saunas where they can sweat, or
Find the perfect, cutting edge technique
That will surely make them feel newly sleek.

7

A husband and wife's shared dream
Caused them to work as a team
Creating round desserts from scratch:
Drop in to taste their latest batch.

Crockett Row at West Seventh

Crockett Row at West Seventh is close to Fort Worth's business and cultural districts. It starts with a circular intersection, from which several streets radiate outward. As you wander off from this central hub, you'll find public art interspersed with a myriad of boutique shopping, dining, and entertainment options.

1

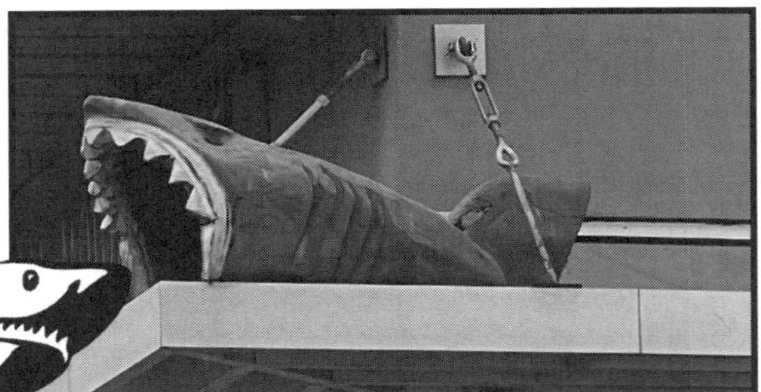

The rooftop shark is no mirage,
It dwells atop this old garage,
Where every night live music plays,
With tacos and burgers for you to graze.

2

This is not just a grocery store;
Behind the scenes there is much more.
'Round the back a speakeasy hides,
Let the blindfolded tiger be your guide.

3

What now seems tame was once risquè
These pin-ups were painted for Mother's Day.
Larger than life and oh, so chic,
As you walk by, give them a peek.

4

Next time you have a sweet tooth,
Look for the cupcake on their roof.
Inside, you'll find comfort cookies and more
At this cheery little pastry store.

5

With its punny name and creative flavors,
You'll find treats here for tastebuds to savor,
Sometimes you must forget what you weigh:
They even have swings inside where you can play.

6

With a smoke in his mouth and booze in his hand,
Up there on his head, a corvid does stand,
This eye-catching mural makes viewers wonder:
Are the birds for real or some kind of blunder?

7

The name reminds me of Dorothy's shoes;
Inside, you'll find charming things to use
To transform your dwelling from bland to unique.
You'll find many ideas here if you seek.

Fort Worth Stockyards

No place gives you a taste of the American West like the Stockyards National Historic District. Cowboys, cattlemen, and outlaws once roamed these worn brick streets, and their influence still permeates every venue in this part of town. You can easily spend a day here. After watching the city's longhorn cattle herd perform one of their daily cattle drives down Exchange Avenue, there are plenty of restaurants, bars, honky-tonks, shops, and museums to explore.

1

Below this banner, you will find plaques
Historic markers filled with facts,
Revealing specs for this entry gate,
Since 1910, it has stood straight.

____

____

2

Cowtown's last major gunfight
With Luke Short and L. J. Courtwright
Took place in front of this watering hole
That sells real Texas chili by the bowl.

3

Since 1907, they've had many famous guests,
Both past and present from the Wild West,
Some say they are such gracious hosts,
They even have some cowboy ghosts.

4

A rust horse stands with a balcony view
Above a store selling goods since 1902,
From hand-creased hats to boots and more,
There's lots on offer at this Western store.

5

Keep an eye out for this name
As you traipse down the walk of fame,
This lawman had some famous gunfights;
His name sounds like he flies at night.

6

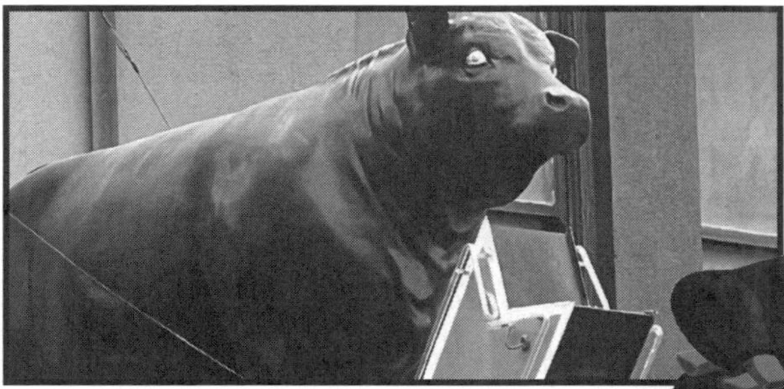

This steakhouse has made history
Over this past century
With BBQ and calf fries:
Look for the black steer with bright white eyes.

7

Look down to find this woman's name
Along the Texas Trail of Fame,
Comanches adopted her after a raid,
One of her sons was their chief made.

8

So why did cowboys use this trail?
For starters, it was much cheaper than rail,
And on the way, their cattle could graze,
It was the best use of their days.

9

This Comanche chief has a statue and marker,
His anglo mother's last name was Parker.
He invested his money wisely and well,
And he built a "star house" in which to dwell.

10

They walk down the street twice daily,
Swinging their horns rather gaily,
It's truly unique, I will opine,
That this city has a real herd of bovine.

11

In 1914, during the first World War,
Armies shopped here to build up their corps.
Such were the times and behind-the-scenes forces:
Mule Alley was the world's largest market for horses.

12

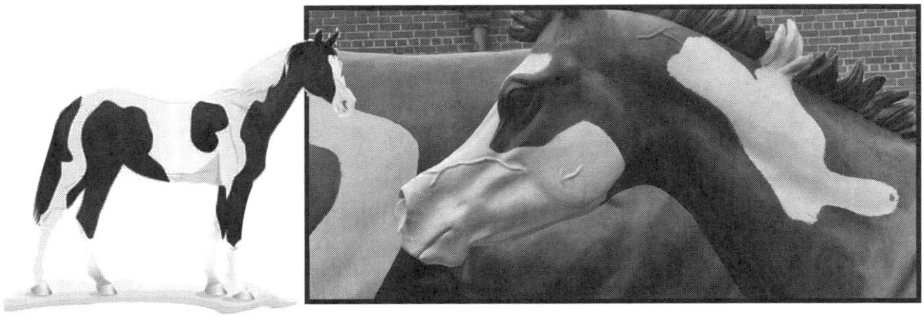

This herd of brown and white steeds
Celebrates a specific equine breed.
In Mule Alley they can be found,
Forever walking along the ground.

13

This cowboy waves a neon lariat
Beside the doors of a hotel Marriott
That's named for the leader of a longhorn pack.
Once you stay here, they hope you'll come back.

14

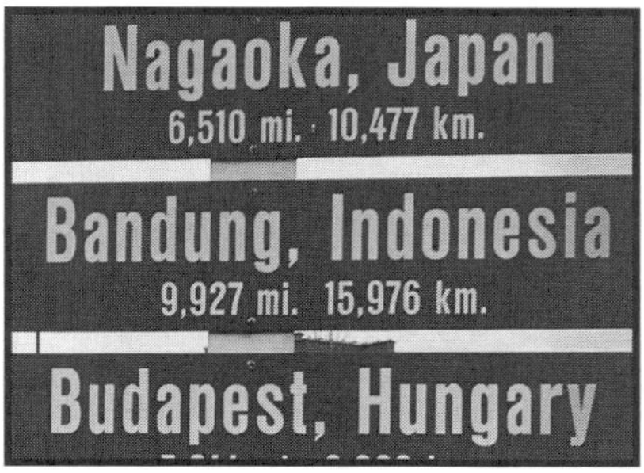

This town has nine siblings around the globe,
From Indonesia and China, to Mexico,
Their names and distances are on this post,
Connections are made when locals play host.

15

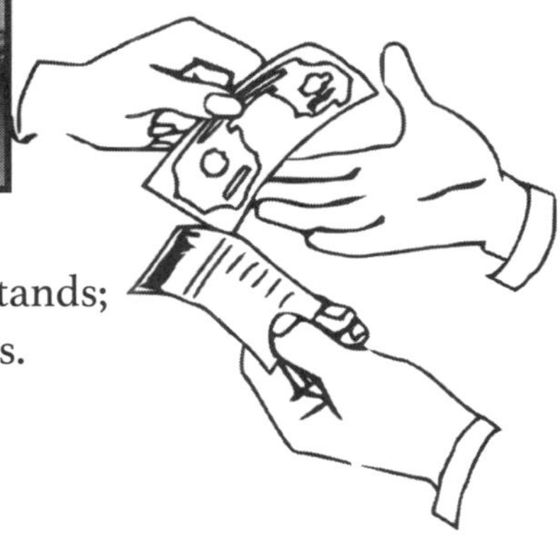

This "Wall Street of the West" still stands;
Over the years, it has changed hands.
Today, there's a museum inside,
Filled with local historical pride.

16

This poet, musician, and actor founded
An event that since 1990 has resounded
With chuck wagons, cowboy poetry and jubilation,
A genuine Wild West celebration.

17

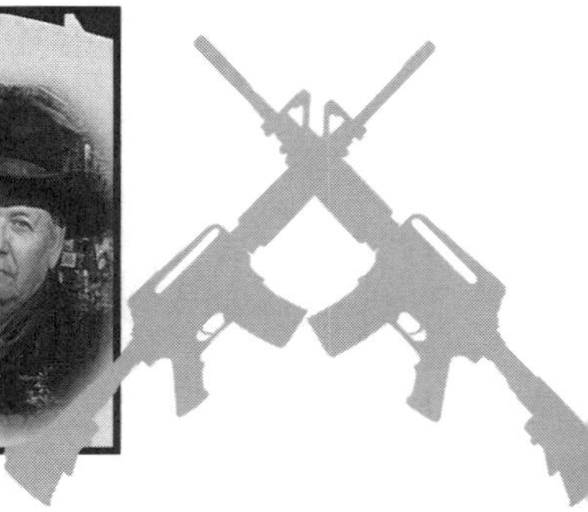

Since the year nineteen hundred and eighty one,
These men found a unique way to have fun:
They reenact famous gun fights for free
As a way to teach Wild West history.

18

Despite its four faces and lovely stained glass,
If you don't look up, this is easy to pass,
It's no hairy spider: it was named for a train
That still leaves this station in sun and in rain.

19

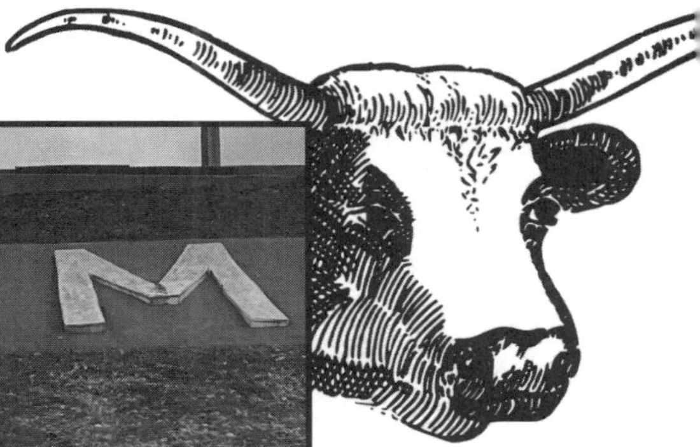

They worked next to the Stockyards, so it only seems fair
That meatpackers are honored in this public square,
See its name by the stairs at the end of Exchange,
Where the city's herd walks to and from their home range.

20

This plaque reminds us of a forgotten town
Named for a man of meatpacking renown,
The "richest little town in the world," some said,
Now it's part of Fort Worth; that old city is dead.

21

For over three decades, it was in disrepair,
Then someone gave it much-needed care.
Now, there's classic films, drinks, and live music acts:
I'm not making this up, just stating the facts.

22

This family-owned shop makes saddles and boots
And goes back to the '20s when you trace its roots.
The items here are made with passion
And a taste for that good ole Wild West fashion.

23

Sounds like a gal's name, but it means the lead cow,
It was once a bordello, but when you stay now
It's an old-timey hotel with modern-day hosts
Who happily tell you about all its ghosts.

24

Flipping burgers was her whole career,
Yet she made friends both far and near,
In her memory they dedicate this alley,
To her life it's a touching finale.

25

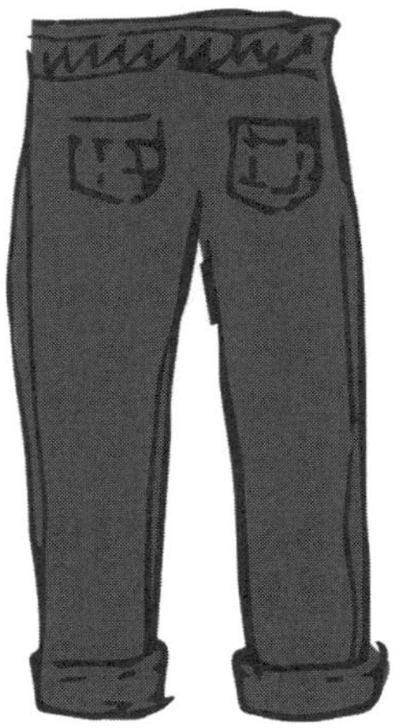

You've seen him tall in dungaree jeans,
Sauntering across the silver screens.
The museum that you will find here
Is dedicated to "The Duke's" career.

26

Much too big for a waist it was made,
But it's a nice place to sit in the shade,
And when you look across the street,
You'll see spurs too big for anyone's feet.

27

This Shoshone gal helped Lewis and Clark
Explore thousands of miles, dawn to dark,
Here in the Stockyards, she's given a star,
Hope you find it without going too far.

Montgomery Street's Quirks

From the corner of Harley Avenue to where it meets West Freeway, businesses and shops along the Montgomery Street add a touch of mid-century style and quirkiness to the Fort Worth Cultural District. A stroll along here is sure to bring a smile to your face.

1

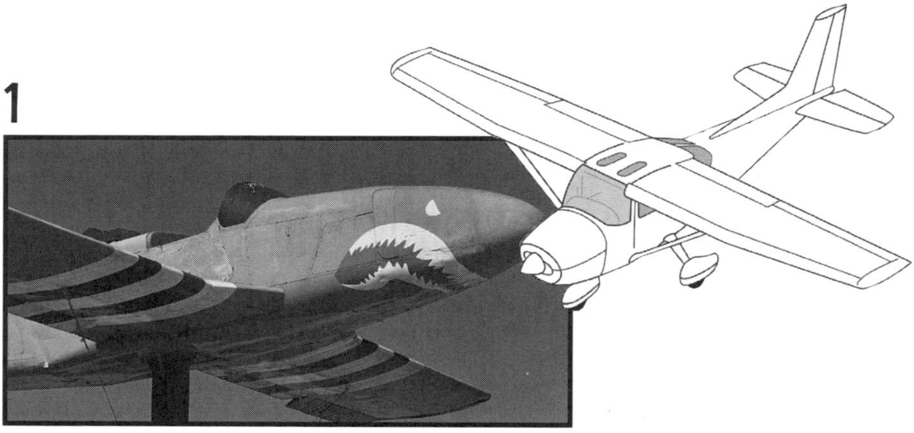

If your "Apple" has a rotten core,
Bring it here to be restored.
This shop is situated beneath
A flying machine with wings and teeth.

2

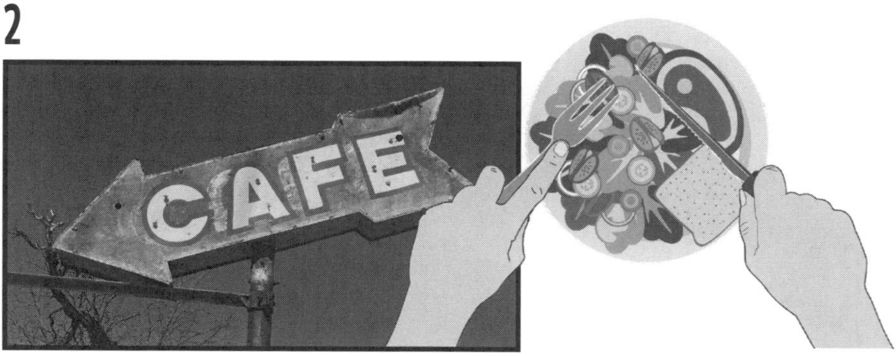

From biscuits to chicken-fried steaks,
You can eat 'til your belly aches.
A mural inside sets the mood
For true Texas homestyle food.

3

Custom footwear is only part of what's here:
They also sell art, decor, and ranch gear,
Whether made-to-order or straight off the shelf,
You'll find something perfect to suit yourself.

4

If you need a shoeshine or custom-made boots,
This is the shop to which you must scoot.
In the Pickin' Corner you might hear live tunes;
Musicians play here on some afternoons.

5

An equine gazes down with pride,
Below, they publish a stallion guide.
Good thing he never stomps a hoof,
For this would surely hurt the roof.

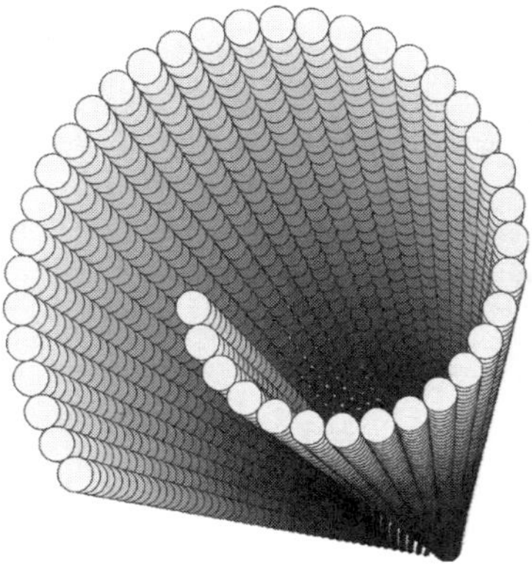

6

"The Tunnel" is what some call this find,
We hope the artist does not mind,
He signed it with a palindrome,
Take a photo before you go home.

7

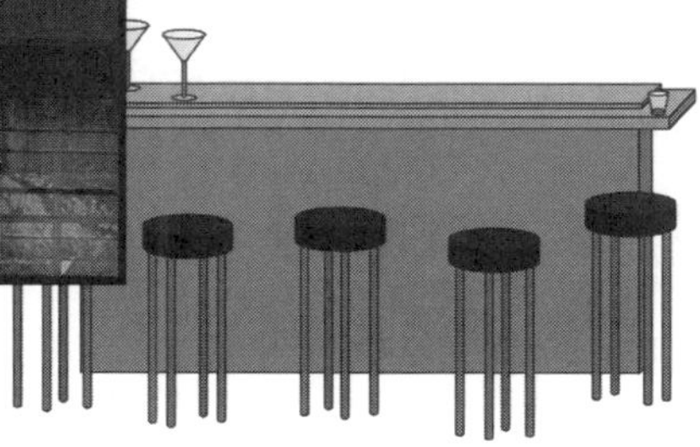

You can come any day of the year
For libations and atmosphere,
And traditions from "across the pond,"
Of which you, too, may grow quite fond.

8

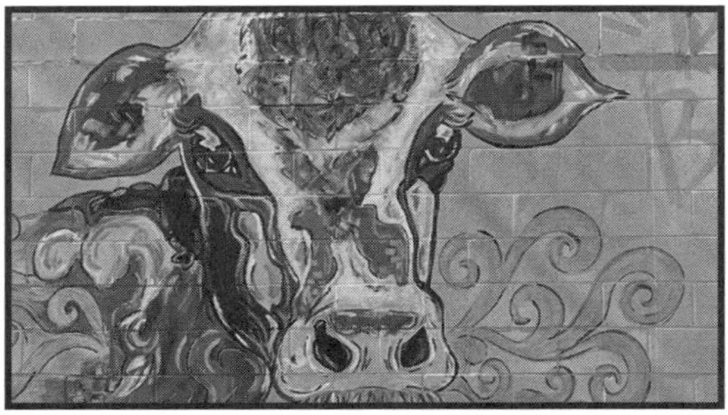

It's not an advertising sign,
Just a colorful bovine,
Which is painted here (not drawn)
With a message to spur you on.

9

The shop is gone but the mural remains,
It's obvious the artist has gone to great pains
To create an image of what's called "break and run,"
The opening procedure for this game of fun.

10

This organization is lively and vocal
About the benefits of shopping local,
For when you decide to skip the big mall,
You support the community by shopping small.

11

Nutsy the squirrel hopes you appreciate
This family-owned shop that, since '68,
Has offered fresh-roasted nuts and seeds,
Providing treats and gifts for your many needs.

Near Southside

As the name suggests, Near Southside is a neighborhood south of downtown Fort Worth. The area features an eclectic blend of shops, bars, and eateries, running the gamut from casual to upscale. The following clues focus on a walkable section of West Magnolia Avenue that will lead you from "the gift of the Nile" to "the city of lights."

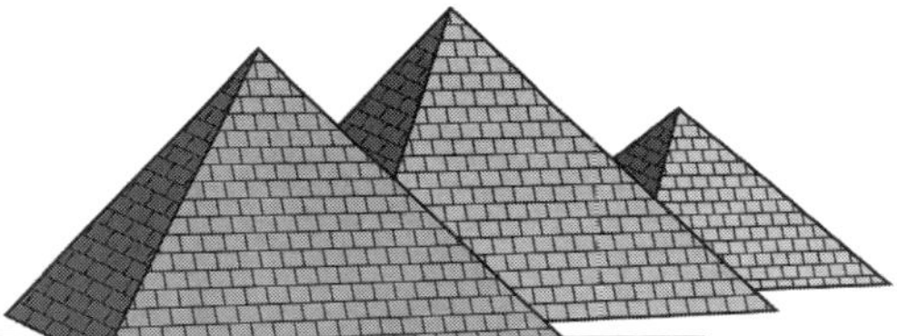

1

Named for a famous boy king,
Many locals love their cuisine.
Whether you eat meat or you do not,
There are tasty options at this spot.

2

All you locavores, take heed:
Farm-to-table is their creed.
They win awards, and here's the reason:
Chef McCook's eats are fresh and in season.

____

____

3

Juan Velazquez painted this with friends,
No matter what skill level they could lend.
It includes a world-famous unibrow:
This mural will surely please the crowd.

____

____

4

About their food *Texas Monthly* raves
So do drop in when true Mexican you crave.
A horny toad clings to their building's side,
Let this purple lizard be your guide.

5

Look to the roof for the world's largest deer,
Inside, they serve craft cocktails and beer,
With taxidermy and a fireplace,
This cozy retreat is a unique space.

6

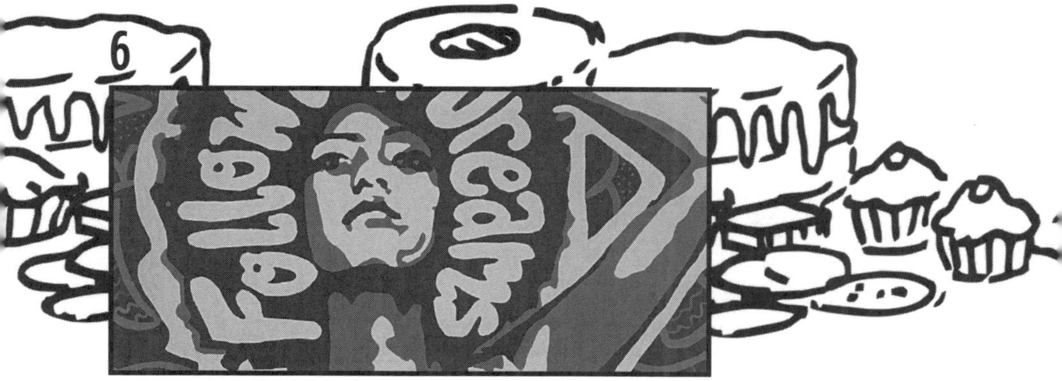

A gal in polka dots stands tall
In this painting on a bakery's wall.
This mural encourages you to chase
Things which put a smile upon your face.

7

People of Fort Worth enjoy coming here
For craft coffees, breakfast, brunch, and beer.
This "locals living room" is here for all,
With a kindly mural painted upon its wall.

Sundance Square

Named after a colorful character from western folklore, Sundance Square is what locals call historic downtown Fort Worth. This 35-square-block district is a blend of skyscrapers and restored buildings from frontier times. Here, you'll find eateries, shops, art galleries, and even a world-class opera house with perfect acoustics.

1

With a hex tile entry and old shoe sign above,
It's kitschy and retro: what's not to love?
When modern developers bought all shops in the square,
This was the only holdout; such bravery is rare.

2

A cartouche with a comical face
Perfectly adorns this place.
You'll laugh like their namesake beast
While, during the sets, you can feast.

3

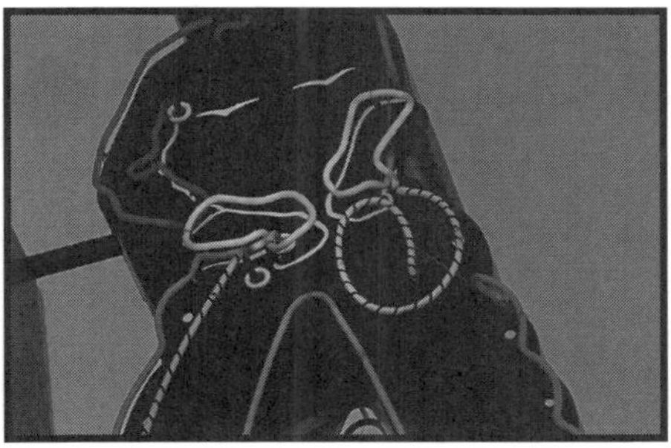

This country station's neon light
Is an often-photographed sight,
This iconic cowboy in plain view,
Like Fort Worth, it blends old and new.

4

A suit of armor stands here day and "knight"
In a niche of bricks at three-story height,
It was erected for a fraternal order,
The very first one on the US border.

5

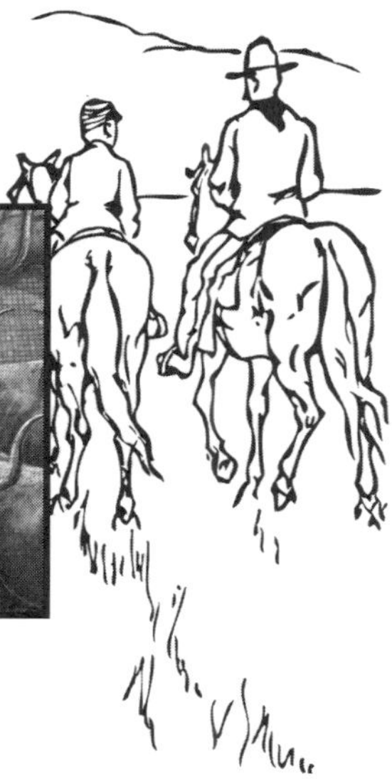

This painting of a famous route
Is large and really does stand out.
Does the trompe l'oeil fool your eye?
It's a good photo op as you pass by.

6

With Cowtown's cattle money flowing,
The young city just kept growing,
This terra-cotta- and marble-decorated caper
Was actually Fort Worth's first skyscraper.

7

The name sounds spacey, but this pub's down to earth,
Since 1995 it's been serving Fort Worth
With over 240 brews.
The hardest part is which one to choose.

8

Angels of limestone nearly 50 feet tall
Blow heavenly trumpets from a Fourth Street wall
From a facade of a venue that's known worldwide
For the perfect acoustics to be heard while inside.

9

Since 1911, this haberdashery mainstay
Still makes toppers the old-fashioned way.
Many famous heads have been adorned
By custom items bought here and worn.

10

A Manhattan building inspired its unique design
With panther heads added to prowl the skyline.
In 1910, locals feared its shadow would bring harm,
These days, it's restored, so we can enjoy its charm.

____

____

11

When these Wild West outlaws sat in their best suits and ties,
They never thought this photo would lead to their demise.
Today, a bronze sculpture that lights up at night
Replicates their mistake and is quite a sight.

____

____

12

The old neon sign's a bit gritty
On the oldest bookstore in the city,
A bibliophile's dream, where the unusual and rare
Are bought and sold here with reverence and care.

13

Here, an eight-foot bronze statue of this head of state,
Whose life ended abruptly in a twist of fate,
To thousands he gave an impromptu speech
While standing on steps across the street.

14

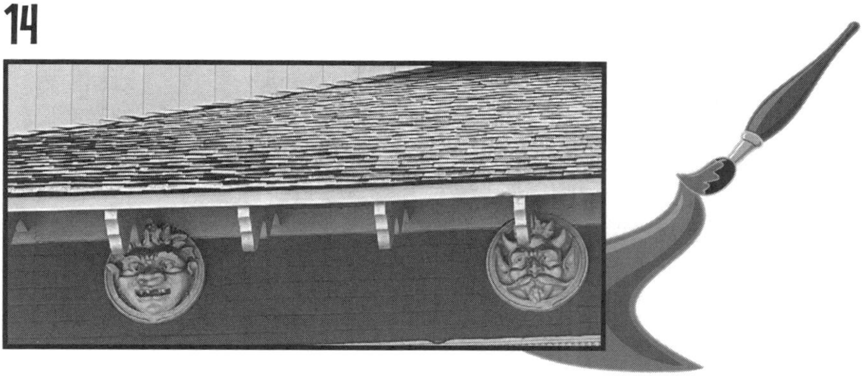

"An artist's studio" is the meaning of its name,
A 1905 building of notable acclaim,
The library once used it to store many books;
A 2006 remodeling maintained its looks.

15

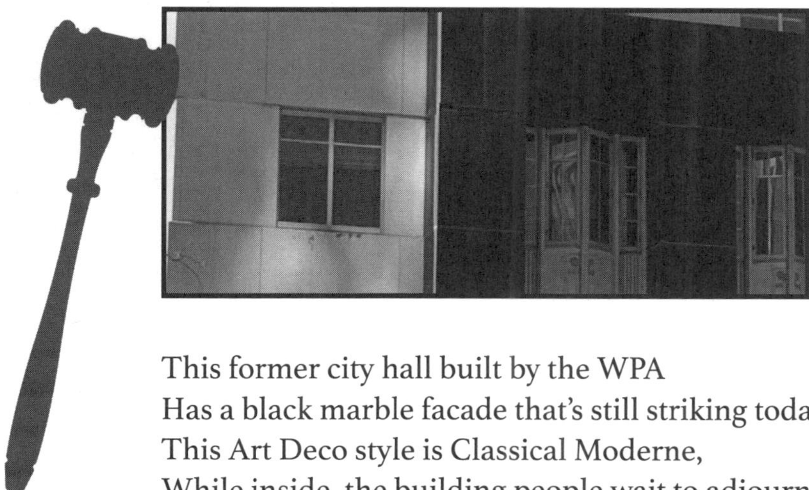

This former city hall built by the WPA
Has a black marble facade that's still striking today.
This Art Deco style is Classical Moderne,
While inside, the building people wait to adjourn.

16

Although metal, it's meant to look like a ball
Of ribbon rolling by this black and white hall,
Its hard-to-rhyme color is certainly bright,
At 13 feet tall, it makes quite a sight.

17

This grand bust on a pillar of stone
Stands in a pocket park, all alone,
This former mayor was a busy man,
His initials make a fancy monogram.

18

This Prairie Style home, erected in 1908,
Was created here as housing for men of faith.
Between these big buildings, it seems out of place,
But it's a convenient location and use for this space.

19

In frontier days, this part of town
Is where Wild West criminals got down.
This historic marker explains
How it got its notorious name.

Metroplex–Historic Town Squares

Historic Downtown Arlington

A walk through the historic district in downtown Arlington reveals dozens of murals, as well as the Stars of Texas public art installations. After solving these clues, consider downloading all three of the city's self-guided art walks. There are too many hidden gems to include here, but these clues will give you a taste.

1

Grant looks happy in this effigy,
Which is how his family wants him to be,
He left this world when only three,
Now a statue continues his memory.

2

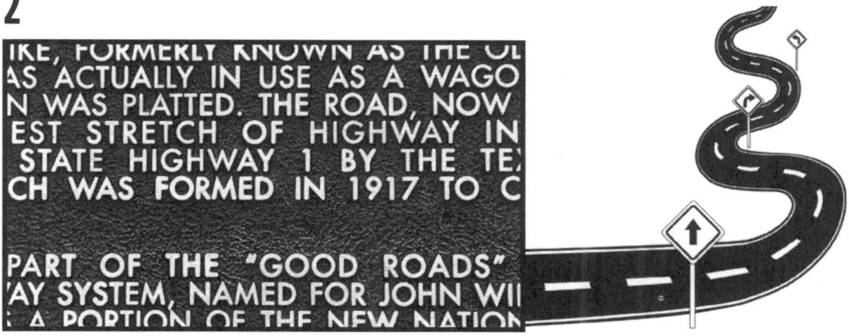

It's long been claimed we can get kicks
Along that famous road: Route 66.
This sign reminds us that plenty of fun
Can still be had on historic Route One.

3

Stone obelisks stand on either side,
While below, regal lions gaze with pride,
This grand entrance beckons all to enter
A street that is Arlington's center.

4

A car dealership and three sports teams,
The Bankhead Highway, and a train that steams
Are pictured here upon this wall:
A husband and wife painted it all.

5

Most old buildings in Arlington were torn down;
"Demolish and rebuild" is the theme of this town.
An exception is the one that you see,
A former car dealership nicknamed "the V."

6

Simmons' design is meant to inspire
Those who see it to reach for things higher,
Even though some days it may feel rare,
Love and kindness are things we can share.

7

This water feature in the heart of town
Replicates where folks would gather around.
Inside each big cat's mouth is a spout
Where mineral water once spewed out.

8

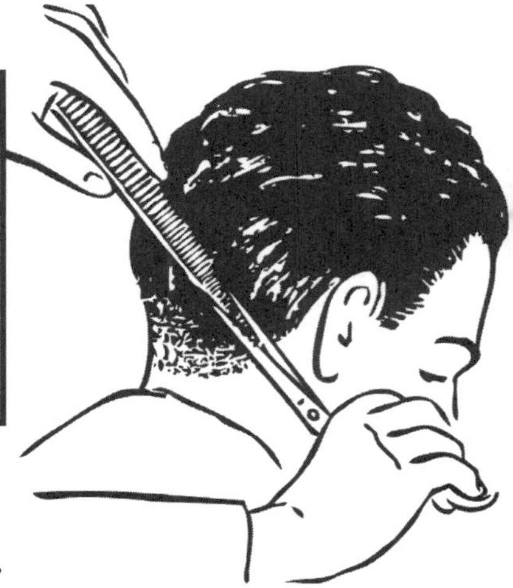

To go from scruffy to polished, just stop:
No appointments are needed at this shop.
The mural outside is appealing;
Getting spiffed-up is such a good feeling.

9

It's a rather goofy sight
To see fungi ride a trike,
Holding a slice of cheese pie:
Since 1974 he's glided by.

10

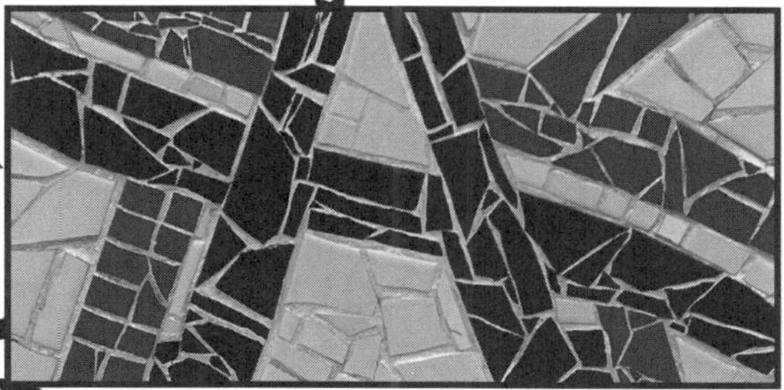

Each of these stars has its own theme,
Representing how you can live the dream.
There are 20 throughout the whole city:
Texas artists have made them quite pretty.

11

Step off the main drag, and you can step back
Into settlers' cabins and an old schoolhouse shack,
With blacksmith demos and a general store.
This park takes you back to days of yore.

Historic Downtown Carrollton

Despite its urban surroundings, Historic Downtown Carrollton delivers small-town charm, with its independent shops and restaurants surrounding a park-like square with a gazebo in the center. Nearly every month, there's a new festival here, everything from a Texas independence celebration in March, to a "May the Fourth Be with You" event in May.

1

When your American flag is old and worn,
Don't toss it in the garbage just 'cuz it's torn,
The former mailbox that here you see
Retires Old Glory properly.

2

Local bricks built this building in decades past,
It was restored in 2005, so it will last,
What you see when you look above the door
Started as a bank (although it's been much more).

3

These five doors were spontaneously painted,
The artist didn't pre-plan what he created.
This mural is a fun photo op
While exploring town, they're worth a stop.

4

For storing grain, these towers were built,
They used to be filled up to the hilt,
Thrill-seekers climb them from inside,
Gazing out at the city with pride.

5

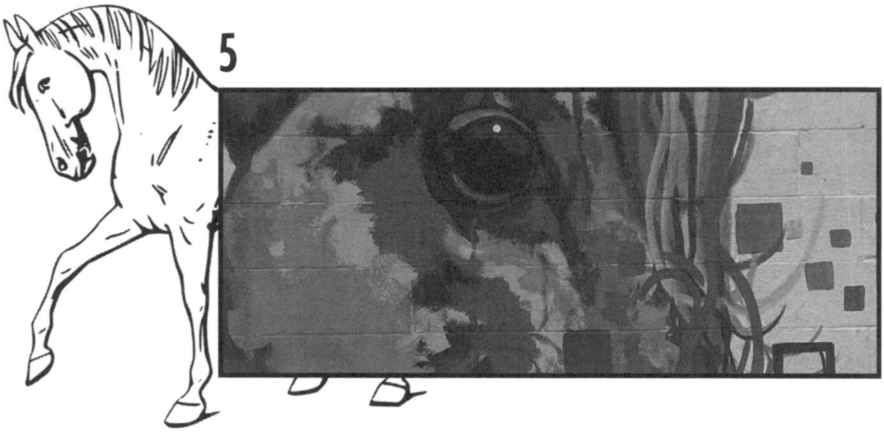

In a series romantically titled "Run Free,"
The equines express a creative journey.
Each one stands for a different life stage
And the lessons we (hopefully!) learn as we age.

6

This mural's beckoned viewers since 2003
To visit downtown and explore history.
The artwork sprawls across a wall of bricks;
People having fun here is what it depicts.

7

Built in the '30s in the style of Art Deco,
Its retro style rings like an echo,
From art shows, receptions, to live acts,
The variety keeps folks coming back.

8

This plaque by windows of many hues
Tells the story of how it was used,
From pharmacies to selling ice cream.
It awaits the next entrepreneur's dream.

9

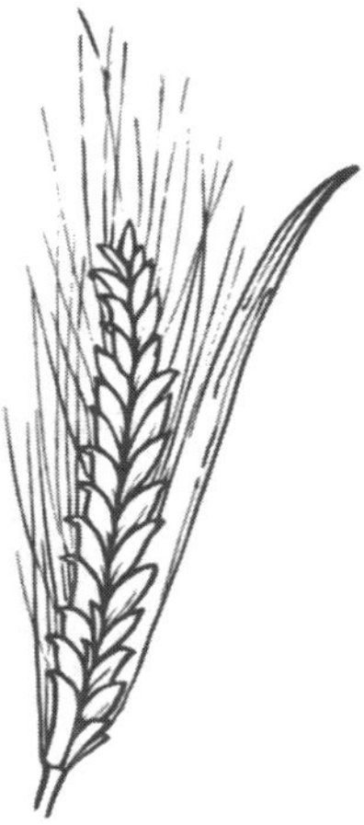

If you pose for a photo here,
Grain silos can be seen in the rear.
It makes for an iconic shot
When you stand in just the right spot.

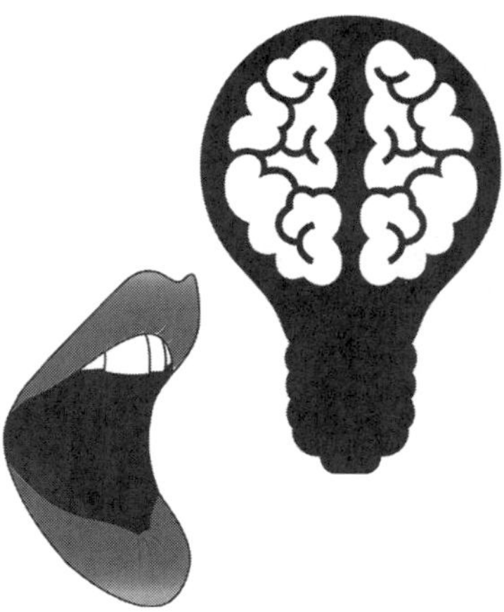

10

Wandering lines throughout this design
Symbolize a full day in our mind.
Thoughts lead us to feelings and choices:
This mural represents our inner voices.

11

Ironically, it rained for hours
While the artist painted these flowers.
For selfies, this is a great place;
The scene puts a smile on your face.

Decatur Town Square

Decatur Town Square is flanked by a host of restaurants, antique shops, and boutiques. In the center stands Wise County Courthouse, an eye-catching Romanesque Revival gem built from pink granite in 1896. The streets surrounding the main square are worth exploring, too. (Be sure to check out the nearby Petrified Wood Gas Station, Cafe, and Motor Court while you're here, too.) A visit to Decatur Town Square can be a fun-filled day trip.

1

To visit Old Town, you must enter
A town square where, right in the center,
This Romanesque gem of pink granite
Is just how J. Riely Gordon planned it.

2

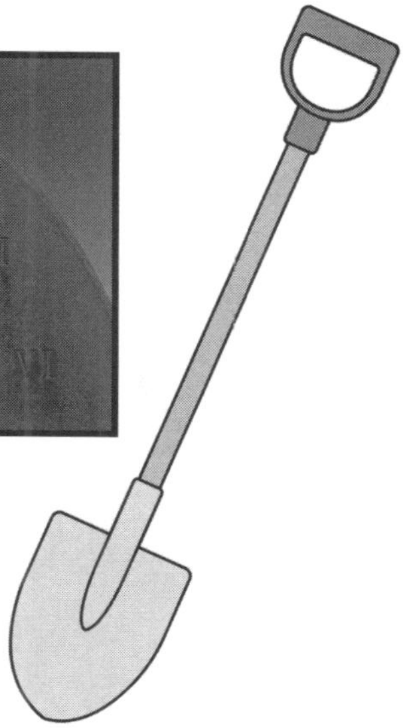

Items are buried here to celebrate
The town of Decatur's 100th birthdate,
It's also a clock you can read by the sun,
In 2046 they'll reopen it, how fun!

3

According to this historical sign,
Decatur was visited by many bovines:
Longhorns and cowboys who used this trail
Drove herds north up to Kansas rails.

4

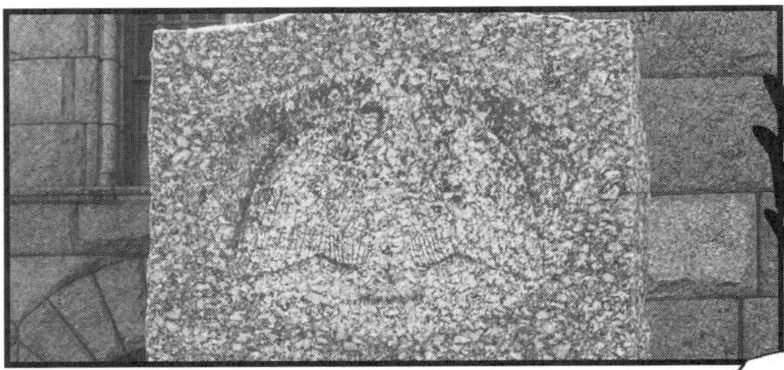

A granite eagle etched into this stone
Reminds us that wars are not won alone.
This monument honors all those who served
In both world wars: much respect they deserve.

5

Before cell phones, these were a common sight,
And Superman still needs them, right?
These days, locals like to decorate
This relic for holidays they celebrate.

6

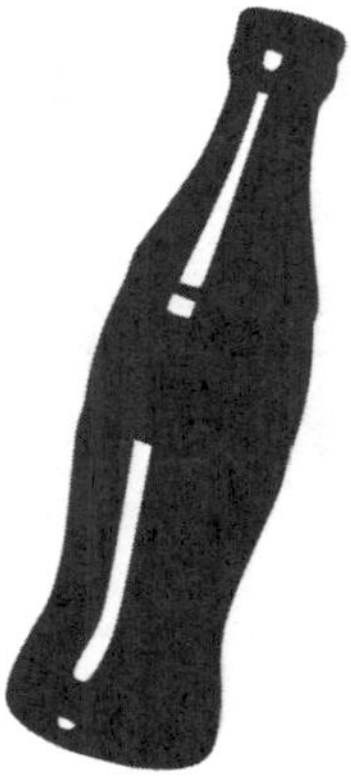

Some folks may call these "ghost signs,"
It's old, but someone touched up its lines,
This mural is nostalgia, but also an ad
That might have been seen by your granddad.

7

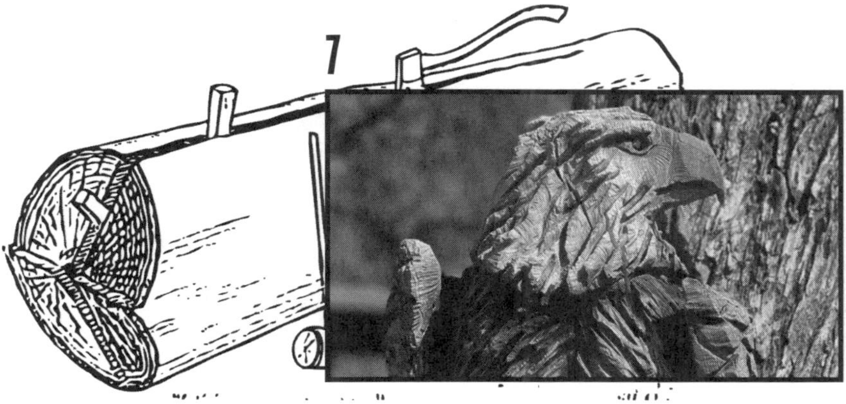

These thorny trees were a settler's fence,
He once used them for home defense,
Today, an artist carved their stumps,
Creating art out of wooden lumps.

8

If cowboys used dinosaurs, not steeds
To complete their trail-herding deeds,
A silly thought, but it just might
Look like this mural, am I right?

9

Here's a fun sculpture that's sure to amuse
Gardeners especially, though it's too big to use!
It's tucked in a corner and easy to miss,
But you could take a cute selfie with this.

10

This steel sapling never needs to be pruned,
On either side are wood benches, rough-hewn,
This mini-park's near the square in town,
It's a nice little place to have a sit down.

11

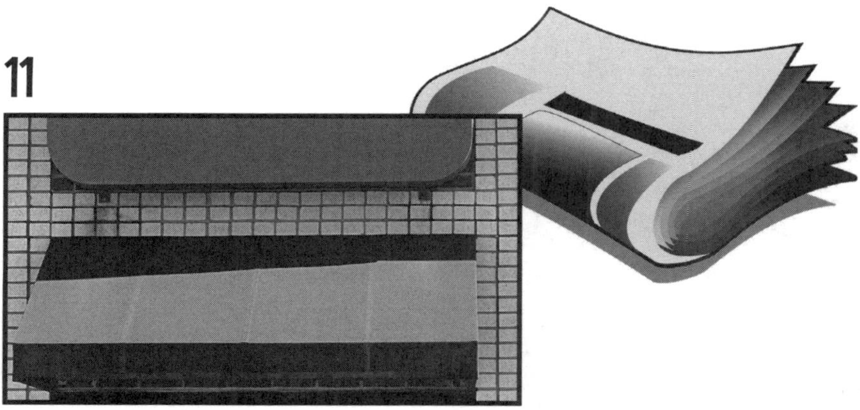

Since 1880, it's been around,
William Forster got it off the ground,
It lets you know what happens 'round here,
Weather, crime, and events of the year.

Denton Square

Denton's historic town square, often called "The Square" by locals, is a lively destination offering live music, independent restaurants, bookstores, boutiques, gift shops, and more. Visitors often don't realize that the limestone courthouse is open to the public and houses a free museum.

1

The erection of this eye-catching edifice
Was completed in eighteen hundred and ninety-six.
Did you know this building also houses a museum?
Featuring local items: history buffs should see 'em.

2

Not much you can do here, but it sure looks grand,
While waiting for the light at the corner you stand,
A classical pediment with a bundle of wheat,
One of many details that makes this place neat.

3

Here, a 10-foot tornado twirls,
Real sticks and leaves form its whirls,
Although made of bronze, it appears to rise
As if lightweight: a real trick of the eye.

4

"Out of this world coffee" is what their name implies,
If you take friends their pastries, it's a welcome surprise,
Even though tons of locals come here,
Don't be intimidated, they will greet you with cheer.

5

In '98 it was painted a controversial hue,
But the color makes it easy to find if you're new.
From a hefty tome to a comic book,
There's much to read here: come take a look.

6

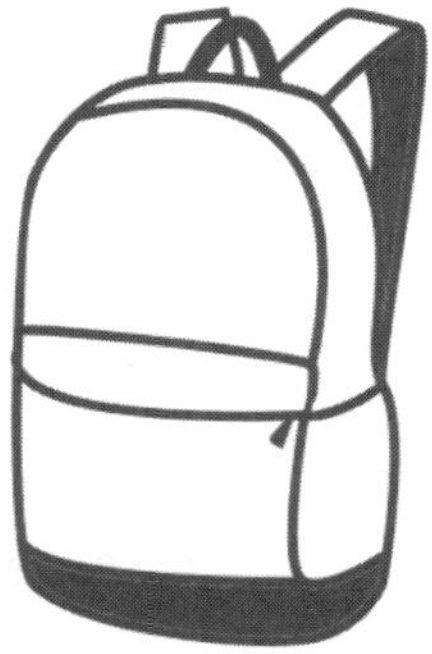

Its name implies training teachers,
Not that they have regular features,
This one started above a hardware store
And gave people a chance to learn more.

7

If this were *Snow White*, there would be six more
Of these "little" men standing by the door.
This one is much larger than most seen in a lawn;
It makes a cute selfie before you pass along.

8

Do you know the nickname for this city?
Hint: Some call Dallas "the Big D."
These red letters have eighth notes within,
You'll find them on the corner, a good place to begin.

9

This was once the place to go
In the heart of theater row,
Now, an orange and blue marquee
Is what remains for all to see.

10

This classic movie house is simply divine,
They began showing films in 1949,
Much later, the venue was renovated
For live performances, long-awaited.

11

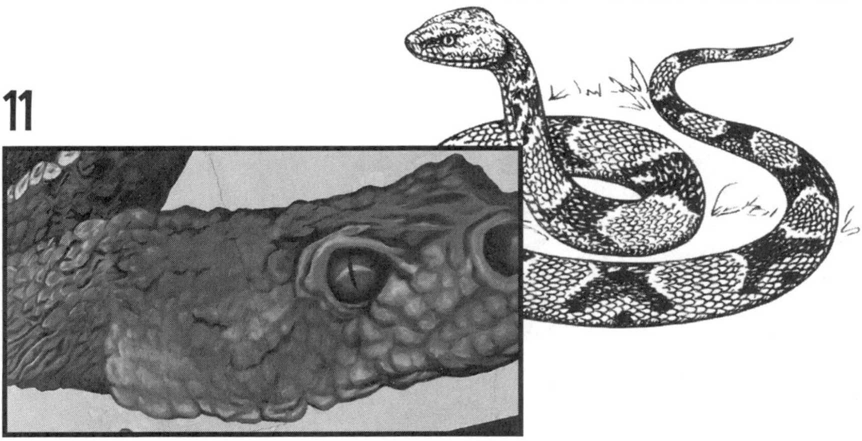

You might be "rattled" by the sight
Of this giant pit viper, but it can't bite,
There are cocktails and food in the building within,
If you're hungry or thirsty, it's a good place to begin.

Historic Granbury Square

Voted Best Historic Small Town in America by *USA Today*, a trip to Granbury often starts in its historic town square. Beautifully restored (and allegedly haunted) buildings surround this courthouse square, which hosts festivals throughout the year. Retail offerings here include an opera house, antiques, books, apparel, and several restaurants.

1

In the town square it stands, smack in the center,
For all to admire as they enter,
A grand edifice that catches the eye,
Its clock tower is three stories high.

2

A UNT grad named Nellie Gray
Had an illustrious career, paving the way
For other women who want to go far,
In 1918 is when she passed the bar.

3

From tributes to Elvis and KISS,
Their shows you won't want to miss,
This cozy venue features live acts:
Such variety keeps folks coming back.

4

An ambitious smithy from Denmark
Came to town and here left his mark
On this spot where the office of an attorney
Is adorned with bovines making a journey.

5

On this spot, two blind bros
Had a store made of logs until they chose
To have a native stone shop erected;
By then, the two were better-connected.

6

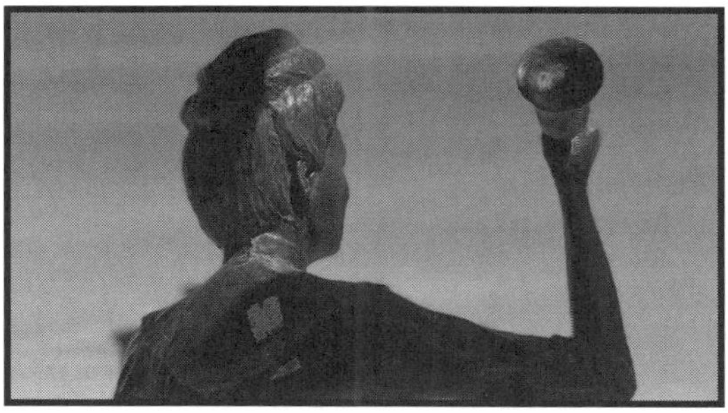

A forward-thinking gal named Mary Lou
Is commemorated by this statue.
This respect is well-deserved:
Thanks to her, Granbury's well-preserved.

7

It once housed a saloon where you could drink and relax
Until Carrie Nation came through town, wielding her axe,
Things have changed: now this places fills the need
For those desiring good things to read.

8

Wrought iron designs keep them from looking bland,
I've never stepped on them, but don't they look grand?
Black metal shapes contrast with red bricks,
When the sun's on them, they look nice in pics.

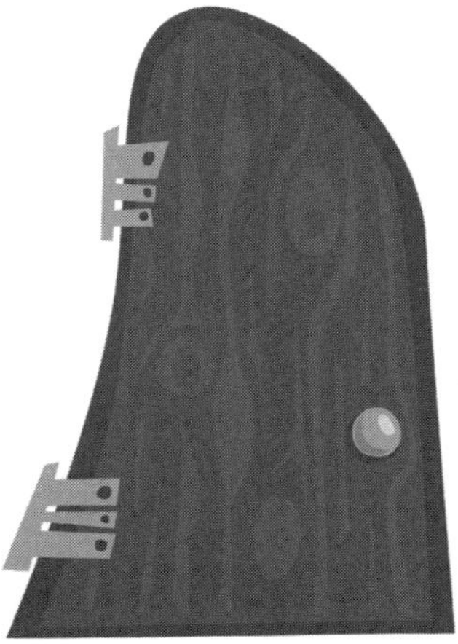

9

This green door is so tall and skinny,
It's easy to miss because it's mini,
Like a secret hiding in plain sight,
It's an Airbnb you can rent by the night.

10

Red brick contrasts with white spires
On this building so many admire,
Once a bank, but after a show on CNBC,
The upstairs is now a charming Airbnb.

11

An artist's springtime scene is here
For all to enjoy throughout the year,
A cheery place to enjoy some shade
Or pose and have your picture made.

Grapevine Mainstreet

Grapevine Mainstreet is a historic destination and home to a variety of unique features, including the Grapevine Vintage Railroad, Palace Arts Center, and a Glockenspiel Clock Tower. Wine tasting rooms, live entertainment venues, restaurants, art galleries, and one-of-a-kind shops line this pedestrian-friendly street and will keep you and your family entertained all day.

1

This sturdy structure was built by hand
For settlers who came to live off the land,
Until the '40s it was home to a family,
In the '70s, it was moved here for us to see.

2

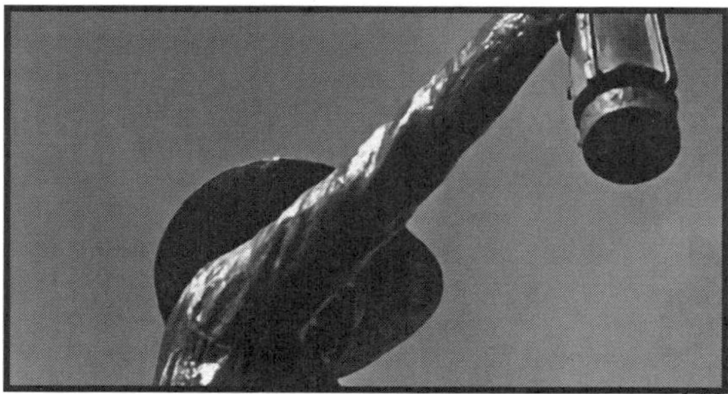

This statue plays homage to Grapevine's history,
If you don't know the story, then it's a mystery.
'Til 1956, men patrolled the streets at night,
Now, they have cops with cars instead of lantern light.

3

It may look simple, but it was an important machine;
Using wind to pump water was every home's dream.
Until the '20s, you had to find your own flow,
If you wanted to live and have your plants grow.

4

This man was known around town to care
For those less fortunate: he was even mayor.
From a South Sea island to a troop of Boy Scouts,
He spent his life trying to help others out.

5

When covered wagons came, folks were not inside;
Settlers mostly had to walk beside.
This fountain reveres the hardy stock
It takes to make such an arduous walk.

6

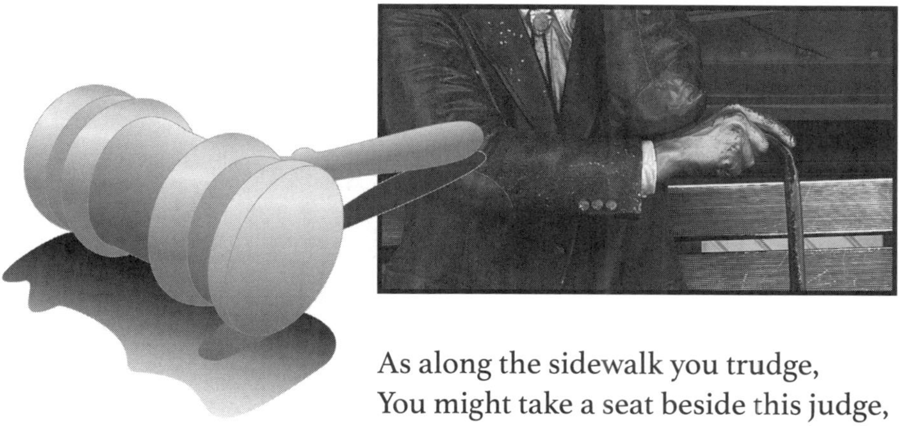

As along the sidewalk you trudge,
You might take a seat beside this judge,
His image is such a realistic make,
He's caused many folks a double-take.

7

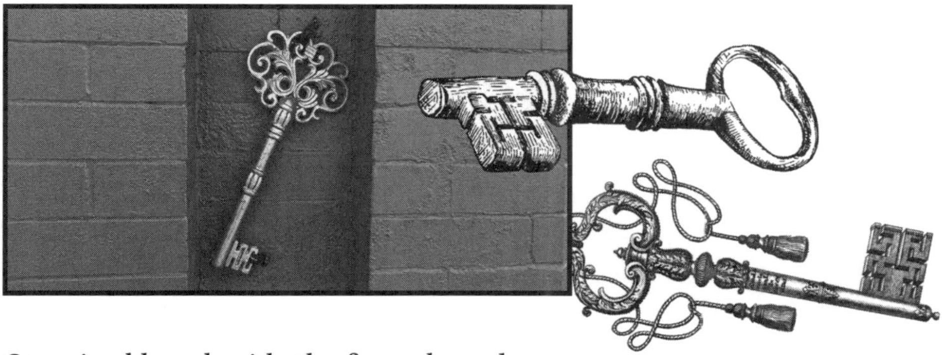

Oversized keys beside the front doors hang
Where, years ago Bonnie and Clyde's gang
Robbed a bank and made criminal history,
But what those keys are for is still a mystery.

8

An old sign atop this building reminds
That locals once kept up through this grapevine,
But now within these same walls you can taste
Flavorful oils with which to cook or baste.

9

If you thought they were rare, you'll be chastened
By the famous men who have been Masons.
In America, there have been so many,
This wall painting pictures more than twenty.

10

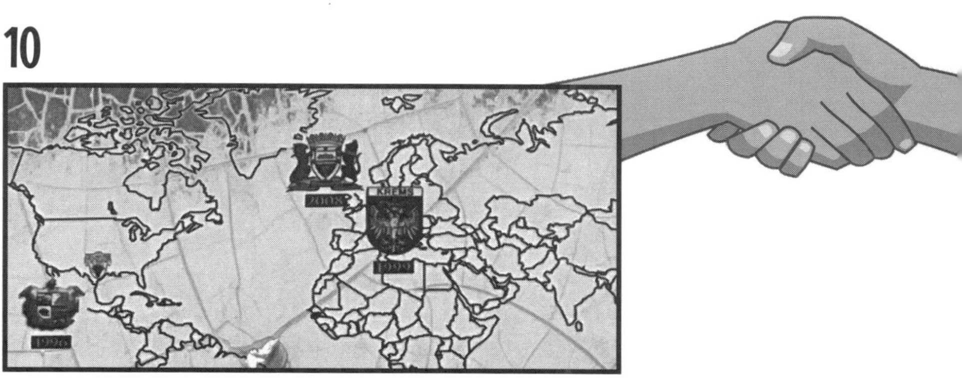

President Eisenhower started a trend
For cities to make global friends.
For Grapevine, there is a trine
Of such towns listed on this sign.

11

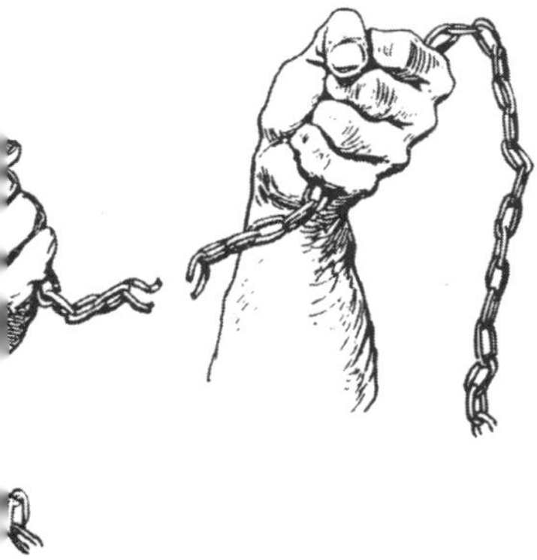

When you look at this shack from 1909,
It's hard to believe it was built to confine,
Its name is the Spanish word for "dungeon,"
I'm sure that a stay here was really un-fun.

Historic Downtown McKinney

Historic Downtown McKinney boasts one of the largest historic districts in Texas. Parking is free in Old Town Square, which is home to over 120 independent shops, including art galleries, boutiques, furniture stores, antique shops, home décor shops, specialty shops, and more. This walkable district also offers a wide range of restaurants, and even a few wineries.

1

Once a courthouse, but now live events
Are what this building currently presents,
Ringed with independent stores and shops,
When you visit you'll make lots of stops.

2

This building is far from plain;
Opulent details still remain
On this Classical Revival design,
An eagle up top and lamps on each side.

3

This fire escape sure catches the eye
Because of the way it curls to the sky.
Although they didn't know in its day,
It looks a bit like DNA.

4

This business is anything but new,
They've been grooming men since 1892,
From haircuts, beards, or a clean-shaven face,
This shop has never once moved from this place.

5

It's large and offers much variety,
You really don't know what you'll see,
The booths can be rented by anyone,
Browse through this place and have some fun.

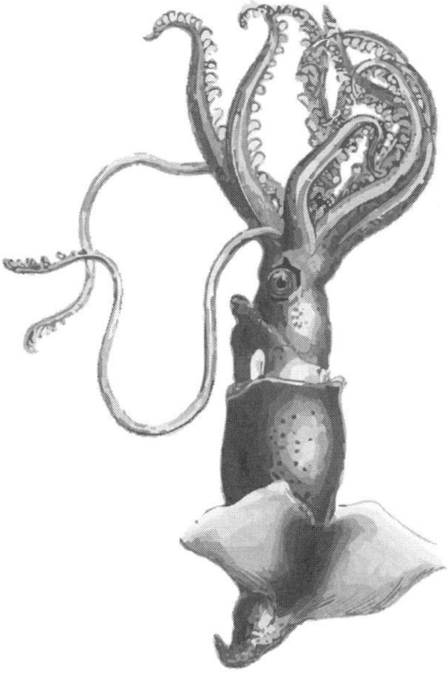

6

The man-of-war is a sea creature,
But this mural seems to feature
A peace-loving squid of purple and blue,
Its legs flail down the wall beside you.

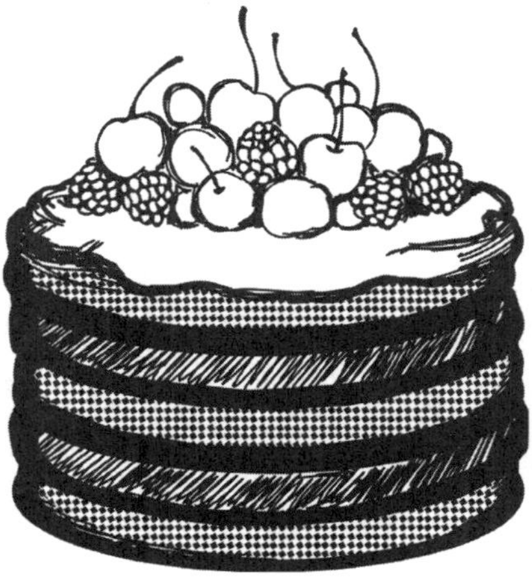

7

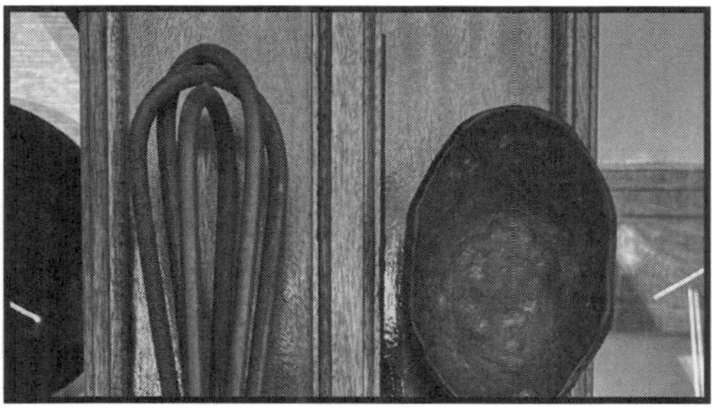

It's a kitchen store no more,
But there are vestiges on its front door,
The knobs are a whisk and a spoon,
Tell 'em Tui sent you if you visit soon.

8

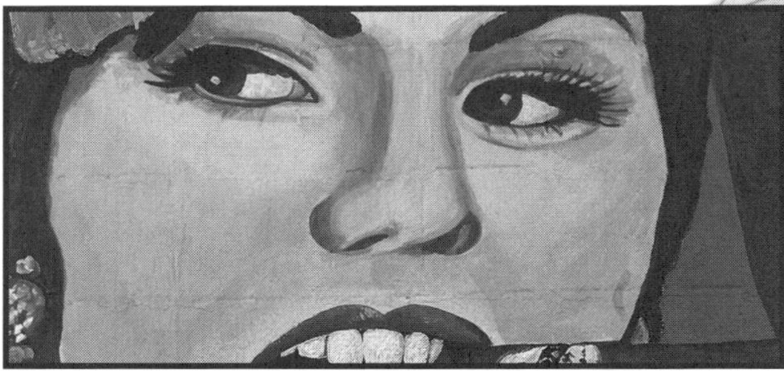

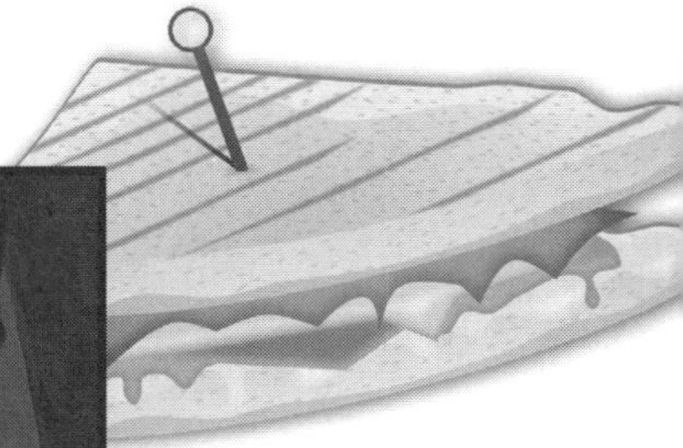

If you stop here for a Cuban-style hoagie,
Take a good look at the gal with the stogie,
It's the owner's mother depicted on the wall,
Based on a photo from her youth to cheer us all.

9

It's nice to read while drinking joe,
If you forgot a book, this is where to go,
In front of this cafe, where you will see
A mini library where books are free.

10

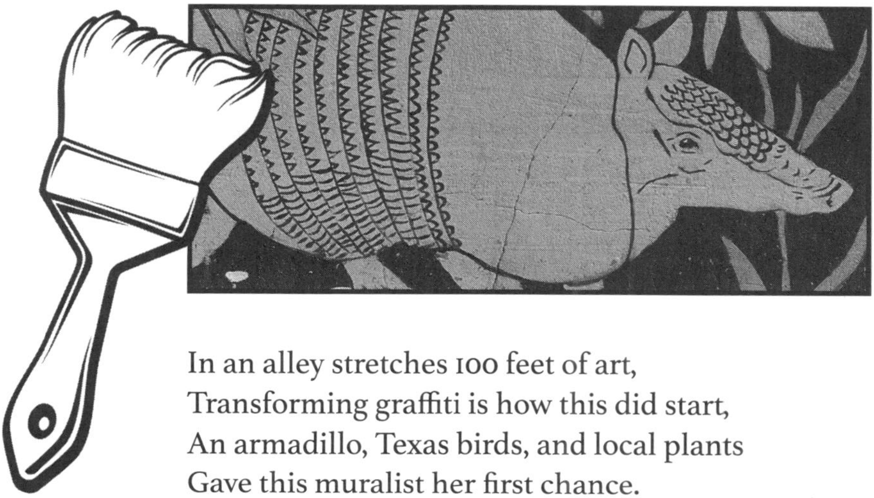

In an alley stretches 100 feet of art,
Transforming graffiti is how this did start,
An armadillo, Texas birds, and local plants
Gave this muralist her first chance.

11

Flowers and cotton abound,
A charming brunette they surround,
This mural has an old-timey feel;
Come here for a fresh pizza meal.

Downtown Rockwall

While Rockwall opened a new courthouse in 2011, its predecessor is a historic landmark featuring Art Deco stonework that still stands proudly in the center of town square. On a visit to Rockwall's historic downtown, you can browse independently owned shops and restaurants. In summer, there's a weekly farmers market and other events, including art fairs and live music.

1

This extremely unique geology
Has long been an enduring mystery.
By the courthouse, a sample can be found
Of the item for which they named this town.

2

This artsy "ax" has a name that's punny,
Its colorful scene is a little funny,
Although this instrument never plays:
It's solely here to catch your gaze.

3

Snip some herbs, they're free to take,
To add fresh flavor to the meals you make,
Have a bathroom break, then take a seat,
This corner park is such a treat.

4

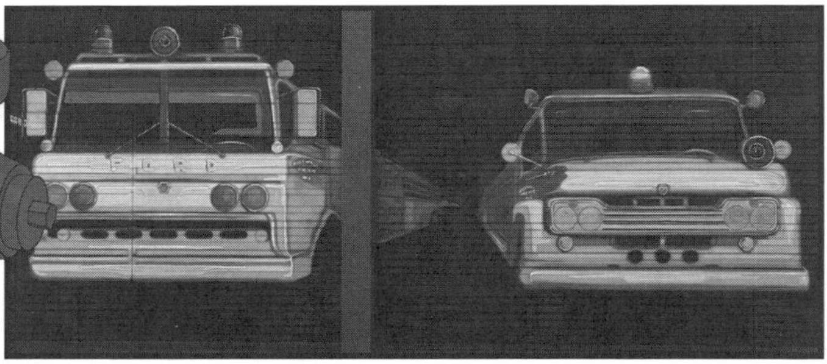

Old sliding doors at this music school
Are home to a mural that's historic and cool.
The building once used by those who fight fire,
Now "Old Granny" and Engine 3 are here to admire.

5

You're welcome to bring your own drinks, chairs, and snacks
To this public square for live music acts
In summer, if weather's nice on the weekends,
This is a fun activity for family and friends.

6

The weekly market upon the square
Was created thanks to her civic care,
This plaque honors a citizen volunteer,
Rockwall's grateful for all she's done here.

7

In the bricks you can see a compass and square,
This fraternal symbol tells you who goes there,
A faded mural with blossoms is on the side,
Since 1854, the club's served Rockwall with pride.

8

With ice cream and gifts like an old apothecary,
This family-owned shop will make you want to tarry.
Here, modern medicine mixes with nostalgic feel,
Step off the square and check out their deals.

9

By the courthouse stands a yellow box,
Peek inside to see what it stocks.
Who knows? You may find a prize,
Little Free Libraries always surprise.

10

Tacos of brisket, quail, and more
Are served beyond this wooden door
With a bovine's face above a tree,
Is it a cow or an ox? You tell me.

11

With food made from scratch and sourced locally,
They make all their own jam, bread, and pastries,
Their baristas serve espresso drinks made with pride,
They even roast their own coffee beans, right inside.

Waxahachie Downtown Square

In his book, *Texas*, James A. Michener described the Ellis County Courthouse as "A fairy tale palace." When you visit, you'll understand why. Start your exploration at the historic courthouse, and along the way you'll find museums, art galleries, public art, murals, eateries, shops, and lots of wonderful antique stores.

1

With more of these standing than in other states,
The one in this town square is especially great,
With bronze eagles and uniquely carved faces,
This building adds charm to Waxahachie's graces.

2

In 1986, they buried items of pride,
In 2036, we will know what's inside,
Until then, it looks almost like a grave plot,
You may even see flowers at this spot.

3

It was once a hotel with stuff everyone wanted,
Nowadays, some folks say this place is haunted,
In summer, boarders slept on the roof to stay cool,
In the basement, they even had a swimming pool.

4

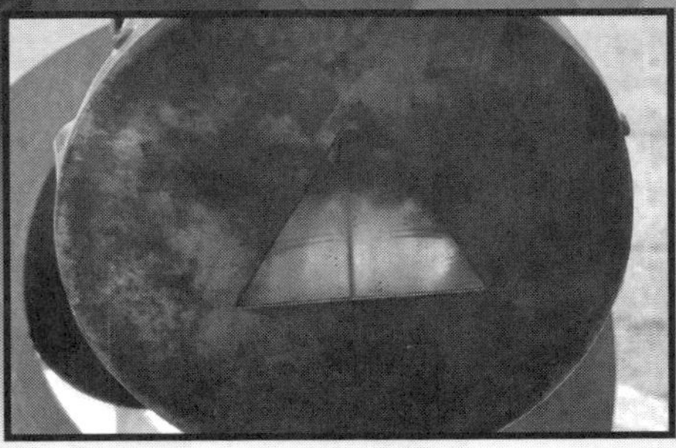

This public art created by a husband and wife
Sits at this corner to add color to your life.
The pair was quite clever when choosing this site:
The artwork can be used by day and by night.

5

It's made from local stone, but the shape it assumes
Reminds viewers of ancient Egyptian tombs,
On one side you'll find a memorial plaque,
He died in New York before he could come back.

6

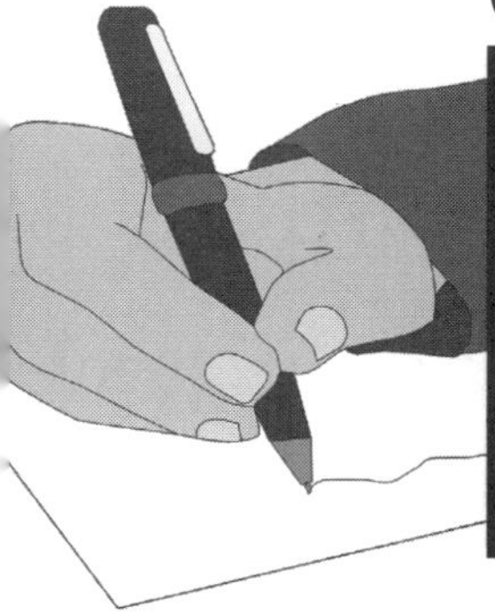

Outsider art and secret societies
Are the focus of this gallery,
This husband and wife's curious hoard
Will intrigue those who find themselves easily bored.

7

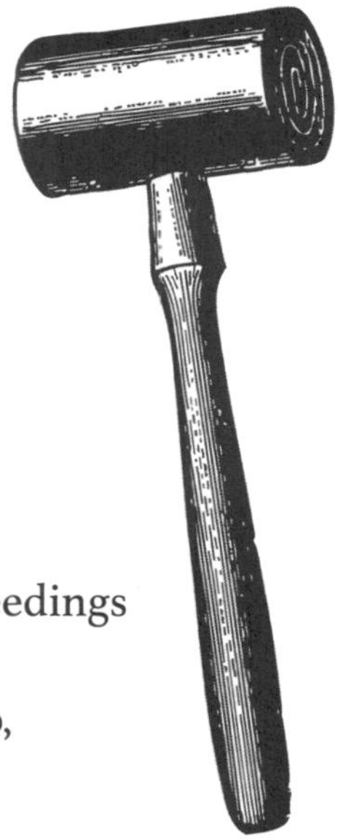

The logo for this place that seats people for feedings
Is a hammer that's used in legal proceedings,
Breakfast and lunch served at this coffee shop,
For many locals it's a favorite stop.

8

"The Hollywood of Texas" is what some call this city,
Many movies filmed here, 'cuz it's historic and pretty,
If you don't know their names, you can get a head start,
Scenes from several are painted on this fiberglass heart.

9

A hand with a heart is on one side door,
A symbol of charity with which to implore,
The building houses a fraternal lodge and antique shop,
When you're downtown, it's well worth a stop.

10

You can take fun selfies in this parking lot
When you stand in the right place for your shot,
Your body becomes the missing letter;
Stand straight and tall to make it better.

11

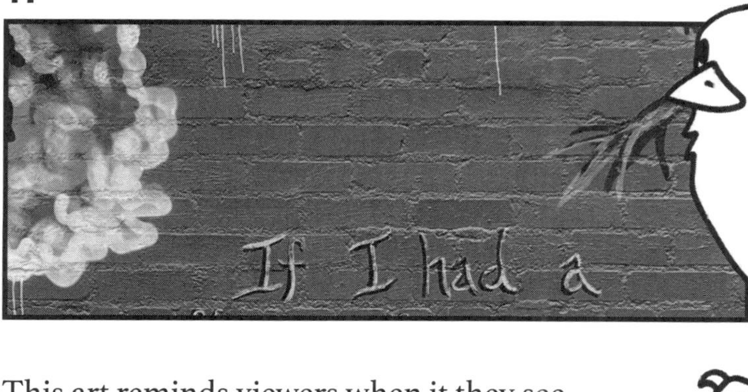

This art reminds viewers when it they see
That Waxahachie's known for this flowering tree.
Perched among its blossoms is the Texas state bird
And a poetic phrase with some romantic words.

Historic Downtown Weatherford

While searching for these clues in Historic Downtown Weatherford, be extra-careful crossing the street. Parker County Courthouse is an eye-catching sight, but its traffic roundabout creates a different walking experience than most historic town squares. On the way, you will find murals, restaurants, museums, sculptures, and items of forgotten history.

1

Settlers once came monthly from the sticks
To sell goods beside this building's bricks,
It's still a very charming sight
When you drive the circle around it, day or night.

2

A tasty fruit is honored by locals each year;
It's a wonderful time to visit here.
This mural celebrates the day Parker County
Celebrates this fuzzy and fruitful bounty.

3

The wait staff have ghost stories at this cafe,
Spirits play tricks but don't get carried away,
For many years, a soda fountain and pharmacy
Run by folks named W. B. Miller and Howard Rea.

4

In medieval garb he stands day and "knight,"
You must look up to catch this sight.
Upon his shield, the three letters you'll see
Stand for Friendship, Benevolence, and Charity.

5

This historic mural by Stout does show
How this building once looked, long ago,
Upstairs, there worked a Texas attorney
Who was governor during his life's journey.

6

In Brad Smith's mural, there is a star
On Texas, so you know where you are,
If you're local you know that, of course,
The steed he painted is a cutting horse.

7

If only these walls could tell us a tale,
They'd have plenty of stories with which to regale.
Below has been a bank, saloon, and much more.
Mary Martin took dance lessons on the upper floor.

8

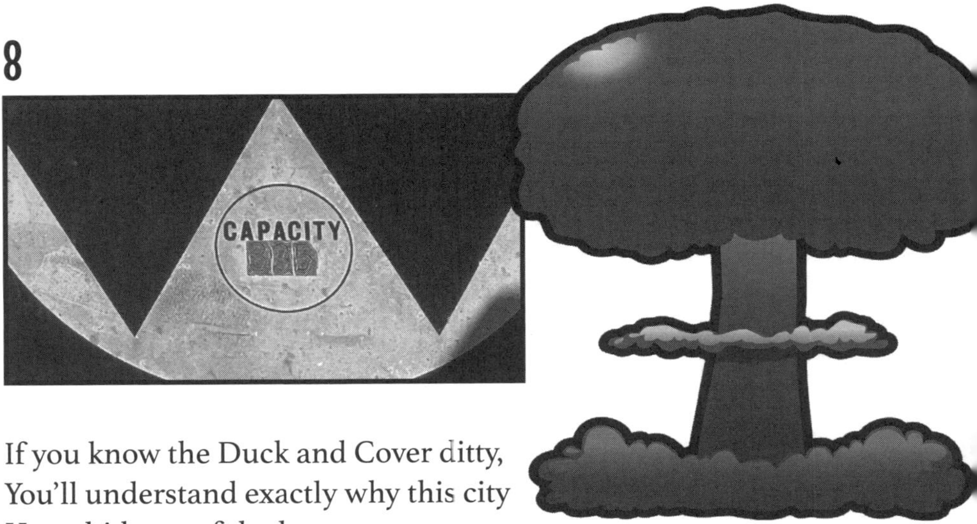

If you know the Duck and Cover ditty,
You'll understand exactly why this city
Has a hideout of the last resort
Beneath the building for the District Court.

9

This is the world's cutting horse capital,
A fact that makes locals stand tall,
This life-size bronze shows equestrian action,
So you can see that it's not just abstraction.